Reinventing Normal

How Choice and Change Shape Our Lives

Darlene F. Cross, M.S.
Licensed Marriage & Family Therapist

Darlene F. Cross, M.S., M.F.T., Inc.
Las Vegas, Nevada

Reinventing Normal: How Choice and Change Shape Our Lives

Published by:

Darlene F. Cross, M.S., M.F.T., Inc.
www.darlenecross.com

ISBN 978-0-9843441-5-4

Back cover image by Tammy Russell-Rice, TRR Photography, Las Vegas, Nevada

Book and cover design and layout by Robert Goodman, Silvercat™, San Diego, California

printed in the United States of America

This one's for you, Mom.

*How I wish I could place it in your hands
and see the reaction on your face.*

Contents

Mind and Body

Relationships

Family & Parenting

Good Therapy

Career & Society

Afterword

Introduction: Talk about Normal

I need to talk about normal. People use the word all the time, as if everyone knows and agrees what it means. The values assigned are black and white, easy to differentiate. Normal is good. Not normal is bad. It sounds so simple.

I have been quizzed over and over for rulings on the subject. What is normal? Is this normal? Is that normal? Am I normal? Is he or she normal? That isn't normal, is it? I used to have a standard answer, one that allowed me to respond but evade assuming the role of the all-knowing Wizard of Normal. "I have no idea what normal is. All I know is everyone has their own version and that it can and does change over time." That seemed to work well until the time came that I felt I needed to take a stand, and I started to talk about normal.

A New Normal: Learning to Live with Grief and Loss pretty much named itself, wrote itself, and just took me along as the scribe. It is a reactive book, giving pragmatic information on how to survive the big challenges we all face in our lives at one time or another. Here's what to do when you don't know what to do. Here's what you can do when the normal you have known is replaced with a new normal you didn't want or choose or maybe even expect.

Reinventing Normal, while a companion book to my first, is a proactive book. It is told more from the therapist's perspective, including many of my own business and personal experiences. It is a book about choices we have in life, choices that create the reality of our present and design the path to our future. It is filled with suggestions and ideas designed to provoke fresh thought, challenge the status quo, and expand options and opportunities.

I swore I would never write a book, and then I swore I would never write another, now I'm not saying anything more on the subject. What I will say is I have loved and continue to love my career as a therapist as much if not more today than the first day so long ago. I am humble and appreciative of the faith and trust so many have placed in me during some of the most difficult times and circumstances of their lives. *Reinventing Normal* is about these people, it is about people like you and people like me working hard every day, creating and living a deliberate life.

Mind & Body

Can People Really Change?

Whether the question is asked with hope, cynicism, or out of genuine interest, the answer is it depends. Can people really change? It depends on what you are trying to change.

Just like the color of our eyes and how tall we will be, we are born with the basics of our personalities and natural talents in place. These aspects are not good or bad, they are just a natural part of who we are. Maybe we are introverted, maybe extroverted, maybe artistic, maybe not. If you compare our brains to our computers, this would be our Operating System. If the question is, can people really change their personality, the answer is no.

Now it's time to add the software. These are all the things we learn, assimilate and practice. As children, much of our software is loaded for us. As adults, we can continue to embrace or reject what is already there, continually adding new information and skills over time. If the question is, can people really change the way they think and behave, the answer is yes. This is the work of Cognitive-Behavioral Therapy.

The next question then becomes, how do we change? Change is hard, and as a rule we humans don't seem to like it very much. While some change can happen more easily, real change demands firm commitment, introspection, fresh thinking and behavior, and much practice to be successful and sustained.

An example of how change does and does not work can be seen with the subject of infidelity. The old saying, "Once a cheater always a cheater," is not accurate and it is not fair when uniformly applied. Of course there are many "cheaters" who are serial offenders, but there are also many people who have cheated who are highly motivated to never repeat the behavior again. These are the people who show genuine remorse for their actions, empathy for the people they have hurt, and the patience to see the process through to achieve the desired results.

The first giant step to creating positive change is awareness. Without awareness, there is no choice and therefore no change. Sometimes it's difficult to see our own software, which is where good therapy can help create change that otherwise may not have been available.

The Mind-Body Disconnection

What do you believe? Do you believe messages you receive from your mind, or do you believe messages you receive from your body? Do you know the difference? Does it matter?

I'll never be good enough. No matter what I do it's wrong. I make everyone around me miserable. Where do these messages come from, the mind or the body? What is their intent?

The hair on the back of my neck stood up when that man came close to me. There's something about this place that creeps me out. I'm steering clear of that dog. Where do these messages come from, the mind or the body? What is their intent?

Our minds just love to mess with us. This is where we store messages we have received about ourselves, our lives, and our world. The information begins to accumulate when we are small children and effortlessly morphs into our truth without question or awareness. The messages even tend to have a pattern I call "YES BUT" language. YES I would love to get that promotion, BUT I'm not smart enough so I'm not even going to try. YES I'm hungry, BUT I need to lose weight so I'm not going to eat. YES I like her, BUT she would never like someone like me. Negative thinking patterns can and do sabotage success, interfere with Self-trust, and deliver shaming messages that can impair the ability to even imagine let alone ever achieve full potential.

Our bodies, on the other hand, speak simple, straight forward truth. The only agenda the body carries is to promote optimum health and continued survival of the individual and the species. It is our body that automatically releases extra adrenaline when we need to run away from a dangerous situation. Our bodies tell us to rest when we are tired, eat when we are hungry, cry when we are sad and laugh when something is funny.

This is not to say that the mind is a bad thing and the body is a good thing, or that they work separately. The optimal situation is when mind and body work together, but somehow these two important aspects of our humanness have become disconnected, and chaos is the result. The mind has too often become a bully that shouts so loud the subtle voice of the body cannot be heard, at least not until something goes terribly wrong.

Tuning back into our bodies as we reconnect with our minds is not only a good idea, it is a critical one. Since it is our natural way of being, making this change doesn't even have to be that hard to do.

Meditation is a great way to reconnect by quieting your mind and honoring your body. You don't need to read a book or take a course in meditation, you only need to find a quiet space where your mind can relax and re-sync with your body. Turn off the "smart" phone, the computer, the television, the loud music. It's amazing how much you can hear when there is no sound at all.

Forgiveness

What do you think about forgiveness? Do you think you have to forgive someone who has hurt you? Do you think it's unreasonable or unrealistic to forgive someone who has hurt you? Do you think there are things that can be forgiven and things that cannot? Do you think forgiveness should be immediate? What does forgiveness mean to you?

When I was in graduate school, the traditional wisdom was that the sooner a person forgives someone the better. More specifically, people had to forgive for the sake of their own mental health and well-being. That made no sense to me then, and it makes no sense to me now. How could such a complicated subject be reduced to a single default answer? How could healing work that is so difficult for so many be so readily accessible yet be genuine? How could there be so little regard for the needs and choices of the individual? Today, many years later, the subject is being handled more often as the diverse and complicated process that it really is, with no one-size-fits-all answer.

A woman came to me after discovering her husband had been unfaithful, and after seeing another therapist first. She told me the first therapist asked her on the second visit if she had forgiven her husband yet. When she was surprised at the question and defended herself as still absorbing the upsetting information, she said the therapist told her the marriage would not survive and therapy would not progress if she did not forgive her husband soon. The woman said she felt as if she'd been betrayed all over again.

A man came to me following the death of his adult child at the hands of another. Urged by those around him to forgive the person responsible for ending his child's life, the man was clear. There was no point in forgiving someone who, as far as he was concerned, did not even exist. He was adamant he would not let the person take one more minute of his life or allow his child's memory to be soiled. He kept his word to himself, always managing to look forward with a remarkable enthusiasm for the future.

How could essentially the same advice make sense for two such different scenarios? How could anyone who has not walked in either of these peoples' shoes be an expert on their situations? As important as forgiveness may be, whether it is for self or others, it is different for each person and each situation. It doesn't happen instantly and it doesn't happen lightly. For some it is important and for others it isn't even on their radar.

I was invited to speak to a large group of fellow mental health professionals at a continuing education conference. The title of my presentation was "Silent Heroes," and the subject was about people who have survived abuse and gone on to live productive and successful lives. As I am often known to do, I took the heretical route and challenged the popular belief that the "victim" had to confront the "perpetrator" in order to forgive and achieve closure. My position was that confronting an abuser argued there was still something needed or wanted from that person, potentially putting the perpetrator back in the power position. I posed the possibility that a person who had been in the victim role but succeeded in reclaiming their own power may not have anything to say to their perpetrator because that person simply no longer matters.

The group broke for lunch after I finished my talk. I thought it went relatively well and was looking down at my materials, cleaning up, getting ready to go. I was surprised when I turned around and saw a line of people, participants, waiting to speak to me. While many scurried off to the most important part of a long conference, lunch, these people stayed behind to tell me how the topic affected them. Several said their own therapists had urged them to confront and forgive their own abusers and declared their work otherwise incomplete, leaving a sense of shame instead of healing.

Maybe traditional wisdom unquestioned isn't wisdom at all. Maybe it's healthy to question "experts," including me. Maybe it's good to ask questions and make your own best choices, especially since you will be the one to live with the outcome. If the result is not what you'd hoped for, you learn to make different and hopefully better choices next time. If the result of your choices is that you improve your life, well, that's the best outcome of all.

Self-Care Is Not Selfish

I cannot begin to count the times in my practice I have explained, and even argued, that taking care of oneself is not being selfish. Selfishness is the most misunderstood concept I encounter, and it seems to always come with a huge dose of shame and blame. The accusation is often angrily pronounced about others, but in more subtle ways is frequently directed at Self.

One of the accusations I hear is that therapy teaches people to be selfish. Nothing could be further from the truth! Good therapy helps people learn to value and care for themselves so that they are available to value and care for others. One of the first things parents of newborns are typically taught is to nap when the baby naps, taking care of Self in order to be able to then take care of the baby. As therapists, people who work in a "helping profession," if we took care of everyone else first and ourselves last, we wouldn't be very good therapists or in practice for long.

Self-care means meeting and embracing basic human needs, such as getting ample rest, eating healthy and satisfying foods, doing some form of physical activity, engaging in fun activities, finding meaningful work, and enjoying fulfilling relationships. This is where I suspect some of the confusion begins because any of these healthy examples of Self-care taken to the extreme can easily cross the line into selfishness.

I dug out my trusty old Webster's dictionary to make sure I got the definition exactly right. "Selfish" is 1: concerned excessively or exclusively with oneself; seeking or concentrating on one's own advantage, pleasure, or well-being without regard for others, 2: arising from concern with one's own welfare or advantage in disregard of others.

If someone absolutely loves to play tennis, then playing tennis could be a good way of enjoying healthy Self-care. However, if the same person used the family food budget for the month to buy a coveted new tennis racket, that choice would show no regard for responsibilities or family well-being and therefore could qualify as an act of selfishness.

Self-care and selfishness are not synonyms; they do not mean the same thing. One is healthy, one is not, and ensuring that you know the difference is important.

Am I Codependent?

It's now been decades since we first heard the term "codependent." The books flew off the shelves and it seemed everyone got the label. The more the word was used, the more vague the definition became. While the concept is an important one that can be helpful to understand, applying it is really pretty simple. When helping you hurts me, I have crossed the line into codependency.

The same situation with two completely opposite results may help clarify some of the confusion. If I know you have no money to buy gas to get to work tomorrow and I give you $10 because I can and I want to, I am helping. If, however, I give you my last $10 and now I have no money to buy my own gas to get to work tomorrow, then helping you has hurt me and I have crossed the line into codependency.

By definition, codependent behavior means the person doing the giving does so at his or her expense. The husband who makes excuses for his wife being drunk every night is harming himself by agreeing to put his own needs aside and live in a state of inertia. The wife who defends and believes her husband's controlling and possessive behavior is a demonstration of how much he loves her is surrendering her power and freedom in a doomed effort to keep the peace. The old woman who signs the deed of her house over to a bail bondsman to get her grandson out of jail, again, will most certainly lose her home as a result of her effort to help.

"Codependent" describes an unhealthy behavior, not a person. Recognizing one's actions as codependent can be empowering in that awareness is the first step to making healthier choices. As human beings we are interdependent and need healthy relationships with others for our world to survive and thrive. Helping others is our humanness at its very best.

Perfectionism and Self-Esteem

"I'm a perfectionist." Words we've all heard often, maybe even said, but what does it really mean?

If the goal of being a perfectionist is to be perfect, it begs the question, what do you do perfectly? The answer challenges the very concept. If the goal of being a perfectionist is to be perfect, then the goal by its own definition is unachievable and a set up for failure. It also comes with a toxic hidden message that no matter how hard you try you are never going to be good enough.

There is only one path I know of to being perfect. That journey is to accept that you are the perfect you right here, right now. Oh, I hear you, but indulge me a moment. There is no better you than you. You are not the same you today as you were yesterday, nor are you the same you you will be tomorrow. Today you are the perfect you, perfectly flawed, perfectly growing--perfect. The lessons you are learning are not generic from a text or self-help book, the lessons are yours. They may look similar to another person's lessons, but similar is all they ever can be.

Accepting yourself without judgment, being fully present in your own life, and enjoying the adventure you are on, sounds pretty perfect to me. How does it sound to you? Consider the possibilities.

The Trouble with Worrying

The trouble with worrying is it means we lose what we do have, the present, in anticipation of some imagined future event that may or may not ever occur. I was profoundly reminded just how true this is when driving down a busy two-lane country highway on a trip in Pennsylvania.

It was late fall and the road was in a heavily wooded area. I was driving back to my hotel at the end of what had been a successful trip when suddenly I saw a deer bolting out of the woods heading straight into the roadway and the side of my small rental car.

My brief glance gave me a moment to slow down and veer off a little toward the side of the road, an action that probably saved the deer's life, and maybe my own. The huge animal slammed into my driver's side door, rolled sideways along the car, and bounced off the rear quarter panel landing on its back in the middle of the road. I was frantically trying to figure out what I could do to help the deer when it stood up and ran back into the woods. Only then did I realize my driver's side door was smashed in and the window frame ruined; the deer and I had been mere inches apart.

People were kind, stopping to see if I was okay. I wasn't injured but didn't know whether I was going to cry or be sick or both. I sat there long enough to calm myself and make sure I was safe to drive again, and then I pulled back out onto the road. My first thought was that I just wanted to go home, back to the desert where deer don't run into cars. As my mind calmed down and began working again, I started thinking about how we worry about so many things but never give a moment's thought to a potentially fatal encounter that can happen in an instant and change lives forever.

In all fairness, there really is a lot to worry about in our lives and our world and none of us knows for certain what the future holds. What we do know is we have today, here and now. I intend to make the best of every single minute. What about you?

I'm Just Stressed

"Are you okay?" "I'm fine, I'm just stressed." Just stressed, as if stress is nothing at all? How can it be that others nearby can literally see there is a problem by simply looking at our faces, yet we insist we are "fine?"

Stress is a trigger, like a light switch that can turn on bad things that were previously left in check, or even invisible. Minimizing or ignoring stress is in effect shutting down our first line of defense, our early warning system.

Why do we do it? Is it the old argument of how others have it so much worse, as if that really makes a difference? "Yes, I have breast cancer but my neighbor has a brain tumor so my cancer isn't important?" How about, "What doesn't kill you makes you stronger?" Don't sign me up for that alleged path to strength! Maybe minimizing stress is a habit, maybe it makes life more manageable, but whatever it is it is not a good plan for managing stress. Whether the battle is with addiction, mood disorders, anxiety, Obsessive Compulsive Disorder, a wide array of physical health issues, just to name a few, too much stress is not our friend.

Maybe the next time someone asks if you're okay, instead of the quick "fine" answer, you check in with yourself to determine your stress level. No judgment, only observation. If you realize that your stress level is too high, consider giving a new answer. "Thanks for your concern. I'm really stressed but I'm working on it." On the other hand if your stress level really is okay, then enjoy genuinely being able to say, "Thanks for your concern. I'm fine!"

We Are Only As Sick As Our Secrets

The problem with secrets is that they seem to have a way of coming back to bite the secret keeper and sometimes hurt the people involved. How often are the secrets really even secret, or are they just whispered behind someone's back?

Our now oldest generation grew up in a time when keeping secrets was a way of life for many. I have heard more than one person say, "Everyone has secrets." Not really. I have also heard many times that "the past is in the past." If the past has not been faced and healed, worse if it has some covert hold on a person, then it is very much alive and affecting the present.

Along came the next generation, people who saw and rejected all the toxic secret keeping. Rather than moving to a healthy balance, as too often happens, the pendulum swung to the extreme opposite and nothing was private anymore. We saw television shows emerge where people aired their dirtiest of laundry regarding their most personal relationships while some host yelled at them and the audience cheered the mayhem and chaos. Over time, the line between secret and private seemed to blur and get lost in all the drama.

People sometimes tell me they are worried because they are expected to report back to someone in their life what they discussed in their therapy session. Screening what will or won't be shared in therapy to manage what will be repeated later outside of the therapy setting sabotages the process and can block real progress from happening. The fact is we all have a right to our own private information. You get to decide what you will disclose, when you will disclose it and to whom you will disclose it.

Keeping your private information private because that is what you choose is healthy. Sharing private information because you want to share it can be healthy. Keeping secrets out of shame or fear, or both, is not healthy, it is a time bomb just waiting to go off. Secret or private, the choice is up to you.

Creating New and Improved Eating Habits

D id your last list of New Year's Resolutions go flat faster than the leftover bottle of champagne in the fridge? Are you already starting a list for next year? Maybe it's time to stop setting unrealistic, all-or-nothing goals and start experiencing small, sustainable changes that lead to long-term success.

Looking at this subject from the perspective of addictive processes is different than looking at foods consumed or types of exercise used. Discussing how to create better and healthier habits comes up frequently in therapy with many reporting approaches destined to fail before they ever begin. For a change, try taking a bite out of one or more of the following suggestions to help you create the success your determined efforts deserve.

- Focus on the things you can eat, not the things you can't. Deprivation and deficit thinking is a sure path to relapse.
- Go to a bookstore or shop online for cookbooks with new recipes and great pictures you find interesting and inspiring. Consider buying some new, fun kitchen gadgets, or dishes. The best way to replace undesirable choices and behaviors is to experience something fresh, challenging and fun.

- Instead of giving up foods that are bad for you, trade them for foods that are good for you. For example, replace that white bread with a high quality whole grain alternative. In time as you re-educate your taste buds, you might actually be surprised how much better the whole grain bread tastes. Besides, no one should eat anything that can sit on the counter for months and not spoil, mold, or rot!

- If you know you are going to a social event where food you want to avoid will be served, eat before you go to "spoil your appetite." Consider taking some of your own food with you so you can eat but still enjoy the company. You might be surprised when others decide to follow your lead making you a savvy trend setter. I guarantee you aren't the only one at the party wanting to lose weight, lower cholesterol, control glucose, increase fiber and/or decrease medications.

- Pay attention to the rituals you have around food that may be important to you. Plan on ways to keep the ritual but lose the unhealthy substance. Everyone else may be drinking alcohol with all the empty calories, but you can have a diet soda with a slice of lime and no one will ever be the wiser. How about a refreshing iced tea without the Long Island? Keep the fancy glass but lose the not-so-fancy sugar.

- Consider designating one or more days of the week as meat free. You don't have to be a vegetarian to enjoy the plethora of healthy and delicious recipes available.

- If you are waiting until you are skinny to enjoy your life, it might be a good idea to re-think your strategy. We are the least nurturing and most critical and unforgiving when we feel badly about ourselves, possibly doubting we are worthy of the good results we seek. Positive change comes from nurture, not criticism. The ideal plan for the best results is to embrace your Self with loving thoughts today to create a happier and healthier tomorrow.

- The definition of insanity is doing the same thing over and over expecting different results. Do something different! Change your routine. Challenge the tired messages you carry in your head. Wake up at a different time. Go for a walk in the opposite direction of how you always go. Think about what you typically do and then do the opposite to create new ideas, options and perspectives.

- It really isn't how many times we fall off the wagon. We are all a work in progress with relapse a common human experience. Energy spent beating ourselves up for what is past would be better spent focusing on lessons learned and then put to good use as we go forward.

- Find new ways to celebrate your successes, big and small. The good feelings that come from tossing that old pair of skinny pants and replacing them with a new pair that look and fit great--and are appropriate for the current decade--will last a lot longer than any bag of chips.

Living with Chronic Pain

I work with many brave souls who battle chronic pain in their day-to-day lives. These patients are at war with a varying number of diagnoses, from autoimmune disorders to neurological impairments, everything in between, and sometimes more than one at the same time. I have seen the benefits of counseling or psychotherapy as part of overall treatment, but I want to discuss what I have too often seen that does not help. I also want to share some proven ideas for getting and staying on the right track.

It is not unusual for some illnesses involving chronic pain to take years to find an accurate diagnosis. Patients may see a dozen or more doctors while seeking help, answers and relief. Some may have multiple medical appointments in the span of just one week. They may see different specialists for different symptoms, as if body parts function independently of one another. The patient may be on many medications, coping with side effects that can be brutal, and too many of these services focus on what the patient cannot do with little or no attention paid to what they can do. The very process can leave the patient feeling more helpless, more depressed, more fatigued, more stressed. How frustrating must it be to have the very things you do to get better and regain control of your life only serve to make you feel worse?

If you or someone you know is one of these patients, here are some tried-and-true ideas that have helped others that you also may find helpful:

- First, do not settle for bad medicine. Acknowledging these types of cases do not fit well into today's quick medical model, if you do not feel heard or helped, find another doctor. If that doctor does not meet your needs, find another doctor. Bear in mind that cheapest in the short run may end up being the most expensive long term if you are not getting good results. There are many good, skilled and caring professionals, but it may take some time to find the right one for you. The physician who is willing to be your partner and your educator and treat you with dignity and respect is the right choice for you.
- Be your own advocate. No one knows your body better than you. No one knows your pain better than you. No one knows what makes you happy better than you. You are the expert on you.
- Resist buying into the idea that our medical system is so broken good treatment is not available. I will never debate the idea that the system is broken. I will debate the idea that good treatments are not available. It may require defining and redefining what constitutes "good treatment" as you figure out what works best for you, but you will know it when you find it.
- Just because a treatment may be considered "holistic" does not mean it does not have value. Just because something is approved by your insurance company does not mean it does have value. Neither comes with any guarantee and both should be met with healthy skepticism. Leaving any positive option out of the mix is a missed opportunity.

- Remember to pay as much attention to your mental health as you do your physical health. The mind-body connection is real and plays a major role in combating any illness.
- Consider limiting the number of medical appointments you have in one week, if at all possible. Too many appointments can be depressing and eat up time that would have been available for positive activities like journaling, going to a yoga class, making a trip to the gym, or having lunch with a good friend. Balance is important.
- I know you've heard this one before: You are what you eat. A deprivation diet is not necessary or helpful or sustainable, but a healthy diet filled with a rainbow of foods that are good for all of us are even more important for those with special needs. Consider including a qualified nutritionist in your treatment team.
- Take a relationship inventory. If you have people around you who drag you down, who think they know what is best for you better than you and your doctors, or who may even question the reality of your illness, it's time to clean house. The drain of toxic people and unhealthy relationships sucks up valuable energy needed for creating improved health and happiness.
- Whatever you love doing, do it, and then, do it again.

Diagnosing Depression

Most if not all of us experience bad moods from time to time, but how do you know the difference between going through a bad time and being clinically depressed? How do you decide if you need medication, therapy or both?

The process of getting a good diagnosis is not as simple as "yes" or "no." Each mental health condition exists on a continuum, ranging from a little to a lot. Situational depression occurs when we are presented with undesirable and unwelcome challenges, but we manage to find our way through. However, you may find that nothing unusual or upsetting has occurred yet you are struggling with painful, overwhelming emotions. Clinical depression can affect your ability to function normally in your life, interfere with your work, relationships, and perhaps your physical health. You may find it difficult to execute even routine tasks, such as getting out of bed, showering, or arriving at work on time.

The general rule for diagnosis is that if the condition has lasted more than two weeks, it's time for a professional assessment. Having a trained therapist as your own personal guide through this sometimes complicated process can mean the difference between adding even more frustration and getting your life back on track.

For the majority, therapy without medication can be helpful in developing an arsenal of healthy coping skills and strategies. For those who do benefit from anti-depressant medication, combining medical treatment with therapy has been consistently proven in research to be the most effective choice for sustained success. Many people battling depression are winning the fight today, but most do not do it alone.

Dogs Daze of Summer

I'm miserable. You're miserable. We're all miserable. Welcome to the Dog Days of Summer.

Every year when spring arrives and the temperatures start to heat up you can hear the collective chant, "I can't wait for school to be out." Every late summer when temperatures sizzle and kids are constantly under foot with everyone hibernating indoors and the A/C at full blast, you will then hear, "I can't wait for school to start!" It's awful to wish your life away but hard not to do when it is suffocating just to step out of your house, let alone in and out of your sweltering car. Is it any wonder so many of us get so grumpy?

If the Dog Days of Summer have you down, give some of these tried and true ideas a chance to help you feel better.

- Get out of the house! Even if it's just to go to the store or get an ice cream, take a housebound break.
- Refuse to feel guilty if you curl up with a trashy novel, take a nap, or watch an old movie.
- Jump on the internet and plan your next vacation. Give yourself something to look forward to and get excited about it.
- Have an indoor family camping trip. Try an air conditioned picnic on the floor followed by flashlight-face spooky stories in the dark. Boo!

- Initiate a game of indoor fetch with Fido. The dogs are bored, too. The cats are, however, fine.
- Hold off making any major decisions, if possible, until you feel your mood return to a better place.
- Enjoy the downtime while you have it because it won't last long.
- If instead of battling summer heat, you live where you are coping with winter blahs, change "A/C" to "furnace" and "ice cream" to "hot cocoa." The list still works.

Never Too Old to Be Afraid of the Dark

Were you afraid of the dark when you were a kid? I sure was. The clothes tree in my room was a headless monster, the cedar chest was a coffin, and I hid deep under the covers so the creatures under the bed couldn't reach up and GRAB me in the middle of the night. As terrifying as those nights may have been, the imagination of a child's mind pales in comparison to the fears of an adult mind left unchecked in the middle of the night.

Fear loves the dark as much as it fails to thrive in the light of day, or even a single electric light bulb. It shrugs off anything factual and frolics in the unknown, writing its own horrifying script. It welcomes pain, emotional and physical, in the places where sleep can be the most elusive and imaginations the most vivid. Fear of losing your job is painful. Fear of failing an important exam is painful. And the biggest, scariest monster of all is dealing with physical pain from illness or injury, whispering wicked threats of more and worse to come.

What fuels this evil Boogey Man? What gives him his dark powers, the loud voice inside our heads? How does he take over the most sacred space in our homes, namely our bedrooms? His trickery fools us into thinking it is because he rules in the dark, but the truth is what he really thrives on is the quiet.

You may be afraid of losing your job, but during the day you also have to fix dinner and help the kids with homework and wash

41

a load of clothes. You may be nervous about a big exam, but you have three other subjects to study before the library closes. You may be battling physical pain, but even that can be lightened by the entertainment of a television or a phone ringing or company at the door. It is when all the noise and distraction that fills our lives gets quiet that our worst fears can step into the vacuum and fill it with ugly and distorted versions of reality.

A preemptive strike against the Boogey Man is a smart tactical move. This strategy requires advanced planning so that you have a to-do list that activates positive thinking and actions. If you are concerned about your job, you could start planning a search process so that you have options already in place if the worst should occur. If you are concerned about passing an important exam, you could find a tutor or take an exam prep course. This line of defense can be empowering, block the fear voice, allow for restorative sleep and a clear direction when you wake up in the morning.

A reactive strategy comes in handy when the Boogey Man sneaks in unexpectedly. This is when disciplining our own minds becomes critical. It takes work and practice, but it can be done. It means creating a healthier and more appropriate distraction, one that quiets the mind and allows sleep to naturally return. Acknowledge to yourself the impact of the quiet mixed with worry is really just destructive noise. It doesn't change reality, only the way we process it. It is human to have fears and apprehensions, but it is toxic to lay in bed awake losing precious sleep while worrying about things rarely resolved at 2 a.m.

Find a fresh spot in the bed, snuggle in, and take your mind on a playful journey. I go through a yoga routine of Sun Salutation postures in my head and I am always asleep before I get to the final position without ever moving a muscle. Maybe you think of the details of washing your car, or planting flowers in your garden. Maybe you go for a virtual walk and count the cracks you pass on the sidewalk until the sidewalk vanishes and sleep returns. If you decide you need to get out of bed, steer clear of your computer or anything that will stimulate your brain to wake up more. This would be a good time to finally read the dictionary, starting with the letter "A."

Time passes, children grow up, fears come and they go. My clothes tree is long gone, the cedar chest went to charity, and if you look under my bed there is a good chance you will find a not-very-scary dog peeking back at you. Those menacing things that haunted the dark, the quiet, of my childhood seem so silly now. However, what is not silly and of critical importance is ensuring that I always have a nightlight plugged in, turned on, and a new bulb on hand. I'm not taking any chances.

A Silence So Loud—Pet Loss

The phone rang. The caller was a woman, crying so hard it was difficult for her to speak. "This is embarrassing, but my dog died and I think I might need some counseling."

The woman arrived for her first session and her story quickly unfolded with horrific details. Her young dog had become ill and she took him to a vet close by. The vet suspected a terminal illness, drew blood for testing, and advised the woman it would take two weeks to get the results. Only days later, the vet called with the tragic news. The blood test confirmed the worst and he urged the dog be euthanized as soon as possible, saying it was "the only humane thing to do." With a broken heart, the woman reluctantly gave permission and said her sad good-byes.

Several days later, an unexpected call came from the vet's office. They'd made a mistake. They mixed up test results and said they had a legal and ethical obligation to tell the woman her dog's results had not arrived until after the dog was gone. The correct diagnosis, in fact, showed a treatable and not terminal illness. Already devastated, she was inconsolable. She was enraged at the clinic for what they had done. She said she wished they'd never told her the truth. She was riddled with guilt for not questioning why the results were available so quickly, instead of the anticipated two weeks, as well as for not getting a second opinion.

While this certainly is not a typical story, and there are many wonderful veterinarians doing great work, the emotions that this woman experienced and described are not unusual for anyone who is grieving a significant loss. The loss of beloved pet can be truly devastating and only made worse when those emotions are minimized or dismissed. In this case, even the person experiencing the loss was "embarrassed" by her own reactions.

What if this had been a human family member, hospitalized and seriously ill, misdiagnosed and removed from life support? No one would be embarrassed. The grieving family would have the support of their friends and family and community, not to mention lawyers. The woman who lost her dog came in for counseling alone, needing understanding and non-judgmental support in a world that too often offers the quick solution, "Get a puppy."

Grief is not measured by whether the loss is of a pet, a friend, or family member. Grief is measured by the degree of loss, how much the loved one mattered to us, how much they will be missed, and the degree to which our lives are impacted.

Grieving the loss of a loved one who lived long distance can be especially difficult as day-to-day life can appear unaffected, until reality pops in with frequent and brutal reminders of the truth. Losing a pet can be the exact opposite in that the reminders are constant and relentless. You climb out of bed reaching a few extra feet to avoid stepping on or tripping over your furry friend snoozing close by. You hang your hand over the side of your chair and find it filled with a fuzzy face offering a toy that demands to be tossed. Maybe you just can't remember the last time you got to go to the bathroom alone. Our lives can be so intertwined with our pets emotionally, cognitively and physically that it simply becomes routine, taken for granted, normal.

Then, one day, too soon, they are gone. The house is too quiet, the silence is too loud. You may still step to the side of the bed, but only out of habit. You may still feel that fuzzy head in your hand, only to be surprised your hand is empty. And you may wish for the bathroom companionship you once found so annoying.

If you are grieving the loss of your pet, here are some tried and true suggestions you may find helpful:

- Find fellow pet lovers to support you.
- Avoid anyone who attempts to question, criticize or fix your pain.
- Make no apologies for your sadness that is just as valid as another person's sadness; grief is not a competition.
- If someone asks you what's wrong and you don't want to go into details, usually a simple "someone in my family died" will suffice, and it is the truth.
- Consider having your own ritual to say good-bye, maybe releasing balloons or scattering ashes somewhere special.
- Put a favorite picture that makes you smile where it is often and easily seen.
- Stay out of pet shops where there are radars that identify grieving pet owners as prime targets for the next big sale.
- Be gentle and patient with yourself and know the pain will slowly be replaced by happy memories that will be yours forever.

A man, who admitted he was not an animal lover, once said to me he thought we dog people must be masochists. He could not understand why we would open ourselves to love our dogs so much knowing their lives are so short and how much we suffer when we lose them. Clearly this deprived man knew nothing about puppy breath, silly games of Keep Away, cute wiggly butts put into motion only because you walked into the room, or what it is like to be unconditionally accepted and adored. My answer came quickly and easily. We endure the sadness at the end of their lives in exchange for all the joy, laughter, love and companionship they bring us every year, every day, every minute we have together.

Everything I Ever Needed to Know
I Learned on My Yoga Mat

For as long as I can remember, I have always loved books. I read my way through the public library and slipped into the classic world of Dumas and the Bronte' sisters by the seventh grade. I saved my allowance every year in anticipation of the annual school Book Fair. So much to learn! So many adventures yet to be discovered! One year when I was 13, I walked into the Fair and was instantly drawn to a little yellow paperback that was destined to change my life. The book was a step-by-step guide on how to do yoga.

First, I was determined to master the balance poses. They looked so cool. I practiced and practiced in front of my mom's giant mirror, but I just couldn't stop toppling over. I got so frustrated but was determined not to give up. I tried different approaches but always got the same results. Then one day I realized what I was doing wrong. I was working to balance myself on one leg when what I needed was to forget about my body and teach my mind to focus. That was my first big lesson. Yoga taught me to concentrate.

I struggled hard for a while as my yoga practice advanced to do the postures perfectly. It was exasperating. It seemed the harder I tried the sloppier I got. I would chastise myself, demand more, and refused to accept my best as good enough until I realized how hard I was competing with myself. Yoga taught me some days are good

47

days and some days aren't as good, and that both are not only okay but necessary. Yoga taught me to stop competing with myself and instead find loving acceptance.

Moving to Vegas was a new challenge as I found myself in yoga classes with so many amazing athletes and performers with exquisite bodies. They were tall and lean and lithe and beautiful! I confess I felt envious and wished I could be more like them. One day in class I was upside down, as is often the case in yoga, and I peeked at the mat next to me that belonged to a stunning young woman. I was amazed at how big her feet were with the longest toes I've ever seen! I looked back at my own short, little feet and, still upside down, I startled to giggle. How absurd to think my perfectly acceptable feet could ever belong with that woman's body, or vice versa. Yoga taught me to stop comparing myself to others and celebrate the uniqueness that is mine and mine alone. Yoga taught me to stay on my mat, and to mind my own business.

I'm still hanging out on my beloved yoga mat. I no longer languish in full back bends, I'm not standing on my head, and there are days when sitting crossed legged is an option and days when it isn't. The lesson yoga is teaching me now is to age with grace, dignity and gratitude. I look back and remember with fondness the body of a young girl falling over in Dancer's Pose, but I do not live there. I wonder about what the future holds as aging creates new challenges, but I do not live there. I live here and now, and everything I ever needed to know I learned on my yoga mat.

Relationships

Real Romance

Discussions about popular romance books and movies frequently come up in therapy sessions. Each person, each couple takes away their own message in their search for understanding and hopes of being understood. Sometimes those messages are unique to one person; often they are similar to multiple people. Sometimes the messages are helpful; sometimes they are not.

Who doesn't love a romance? In a television interview with James Cameron, he pointed out the first two hours of his blockbuster movie version of Titanic weren't even about the ship. How exciting to watch the desperate heroin as she runs to leap to her death only to be rescued by the handsome young stranger. How titillating to observe the growing sexual tension as the romance unfolds leading to the inevitable sex scene, complete with steamed up windows and plenty of imagination to fill in all the details. Spice it all up with a dash of rebellion, and oh what a ride!

But, what if the ship hadn't sunk? What if Rose and Jack had walked off the ship, hand in hand, and into the reality of their dreams of a future together? Rose's solution to her contempt for her life of privilege, her annoying mother and her overbearing fiancé, was to leap from the ship into the abyss of the frigid North Atlantic Ocean. The audience will never know if she would have followed through or not without Jack's flirtatious intervention. And who flirts with a woman about to kill herself? Well, in this story, an unemployed man who won his last-minute ticket in a game of poker with some drinking buddies, off to his next adventure. You see where I'm going with this.

Don't get me wrong, it's not that as a couples' therapist I don't love romance. It is that I love great romance. First loves, young loves, new loves are amazing, intoxicating, but what about creating a lifetime with the person you fell in love with and sincerely promised until death do you part?

What if real love looks less like Jack and Rose on the ill-fated Titanic and more like the characters in the movie *Hope Springs*, stunningly played by Meryl Streep and Tommy Lee Jones? What if our bodies change over time, we have to go to work every day, we wake up grumpy with bad breath, and sex becomes a routine? What if real romance is a marathon and not a sprint? Isn't that what we really want? Don't most if not all of us want to wake up next to our best friend, know they have our back no matter what, love our children as much as we do—even when they are being the most unlovable? Don't we want to someday take turns bouncing our grandchildren on our knees?

Real romance is quiet. It is private and cherished between two people. It lacks the drama to become a blockbuster novel or movie or a soap opera anyone would care enough about to watch. It is not a matter of luck and may look easy to those nearby, but it is the result of much hard work and devotion, compromise and commitment, during the best and the worst of times. Romantic love is a lot of fun, but real love is for real grown-ups.

Conflict in Marriage Quiz

Question: What is the most reported reason marriages fail?
Most Common Answer: Money.
Question: What is the real reason why marriages fail?
Correct Answer: Competition.

The most popular belief about the source of conflict in relationships, money, isn't about money at all. It is about the distribution of power in a relationship, and money is simply the language of the conflict.

Couples that manage their combined finances by mutual agreement are working as a team, even if the agreement is that one partner will take full responsibility and the other none. On the contrary, a couple where one partner dominates the control of the finances while the other meekly or resentfully submits, represents an out-of-balance system that is guaranteed to cause problems. For example, the controlling partner may assume the parent role over the submissive partner, creating a parent-child dynamic instead of adult-to-adult interaction. The submissive partner may secretly spend money or stash cash covertly, assuming the child role and behaving in a passive-aggressive manner. Whatever the subject--money, where you go for vacation, which side of the family you spend the holidays with, who initiates sex--this same assessment pattern can be applied.

So, who wins this competition in the game of control? If your winning means your spouse or partner loses, how can you win? When I first point out a competitive pattern to a couple demonstrating these behaviors, I am often met with resistance and denial. Answering a few simple questions tends to be revealing. Who decided how you will do this? How did you decide? What happens when you disagree?

The wife of one couple was always frustrated over carrying the majority of responsibility for cleaning the house. It was the source of many arguments in the marriage, fueled by the fact both held full-time jobs outside of the home. Beyond frustrated one day she blurted out, "I HATE to run the vacuum cleaner! I'd rather clean the whole house twice than run the stinking vacuum cleaner once!" The husband seemed somewhat surprised and calmly replied, "I kind of like running the vacuum cleaner." They made a team decision that worked from that day forward that the wife cleaned and the husband vacuumed, and the resolved conflict was never an issue again.

Clarify to Communicate

"We just don't communicate!"

How many times have we all heard that lament? The truth is you are always communicating, even if no one is saying a word. Crossing your arms with a scowl on your face is communicating. Walking out the door in the middle of an argument is communicating. A gentle kiss on the cheek says a lot.

A major deterrent to effective communication is failing to first clarify the subject and both people's positions before launching into the discussion. Often one person assumes what the other thinks and means and proceeds as if they have the facts, without ever verifying the information. It's possible both parties could be engaged in a dialogue without even knowing they aren't talking about the same thing.

My oldest son brought my little granddaughter cross country for her first visit. We were amazed at how easily she settled in, as if she'd lived here all her life. It was Father's Day weekend and she kept saying that she wasn't going home until "fall." At first we thought the "fall" comments were cute, but I could see my son becoming increasingly more uncomfortable with each repetition. I later heard him on the phone with his wife in a concerned voice saying, "Yeah, she says she isn't coming home until fall." That's when I decided an intervention was needed. I simply asked my granddaughter so both her parents could hear, "Honey, when is fall?" Without a second's hesitation, she innocently but confidently responded, "In three days." Three days was exactly the length of their visit.

Take the time to make sure you clearly understand your situation and the subject at hand first before you react. Taking those few extra minutes to confirm you are on the right track is guaranteed to help improve your communications, allows the other person to feel heard, and increases the chance you will create the outcome you desire.

Making Relationships Work

I participated in a project several years ago that focused on how people are attracted to one another in romantic relationships. It was a natural extension of other work I was doing at the time, teaching a dating workshop and leading a support group for newly-single people looking to find and be healthier in new relationships.

I read extensive research, looked at all the popular dating services' matching systems and procedures, and I talked to many people. Mostly I observed the couples I was working with to isolate what differentiated the couples who stayed together from those that did not. What I observed consistently was that the single most important factor related to success was commitment to the relationship and to the partner or spouse.

A personality assessment completed with one highly conflicted couple revealed their compatibility to be truly outstanding (Myers-Briggs Type Indicator). Any matchmaker or dating site would have had a winner on their hands with this one. The husband was thrilled and wanted to continue therapy unlike the wife who was not thrilled and was determined she wanted a divorce. Contrast this case to many where the two people have low compatibility scores yet sustain long, loving relationships where the word "divorce" is never spoken. The difference is commitment.

Chemistry is what attracts two people. Infatuation is the excitement that fuels a new relationship and moves it forward.

Commitment is the key ingredient on the path to a long and happy life together.

Growth through Conflict

M any if not most people will do anything to avoid conflict. The problem with avoidance is that healthy conflict, unlike toxic conflict, is a great way to grow a relationship. Every conflict avoided is another missed opportunity for creating stronger connections with important people in our lives.

If two people engage in toxic conflict, they might demean one another or engage in personal attacks, not addressing the real issue or issues at hand. One or both parties may assume a superior stance over the other, as if there is only one correct position to take or opinion to have. Maybe one or both people walk out on the other in a passive-aggressive or hostile manner, demonstrating a power play rather than seeking compromise or resolution.

On the other hand, healthy conflict means both people carefully and respectfully listen to each other to identify exactly where opinions or positions differ. One would listen to what makes the other think and feel as he or she does, and then the other would do the same in turn. Both would likely then work toward further clarification and hopefully end up agreeing or agreeing to disagree. The end result is each has a new understanding of the other that could never have been achieved without having the discussion and addressing the conflict.

Often people will avoid conflict out of fear that to address it will damage their relationship. Of course there is always that risk whenever we make ourselves vulnerable to another person. However, maybe what should be feared more is the damage caused to a relationship by unspoken and unresolved conflict, repeatedly surfacing because problems were never put to rest.

Learning healthy conflict skills takes effort, practice, and a willingness to keep trying even after making mistakes--no different from learning new skills in anything. Being willing and able to engage in healthy conflict can pay off in every aspect of life and every relationship encountered. Imagine what your job, your family, your community, your life, our world might look like if everyone listened, put personal agendas aside, and treated others with dignity and respect. Just imagine.

Celebrity Divorces

What is the fascination with celebrity divorces? How do they get top billing in the news as if each was the first, not just the latest? It's hard to believe anyone can be surprised, yet the public's fascination doesn't seem to dissipate with each new break up. How could divorce still be so interesting in this day and age?

No one can say for certain what makes these stories so newsworthy. Maybe it's the idea that if celebrity marriages with all their fame, beauty and fortune can implode, the rest of us are easily justified in having the same thing happen to us. Maybe it's like driving by an accident and looking even though we know we shouldn't. Maybe it's that we just need the distraction from the daily grind and challenges of life.

What we can say with relative certainty is that too much of anything is too much. When a celebrity is declaring his undying love and devotion while acting like a monkey on national television, it's too much. When a married couple who happen to be celebrities can't keep their hands off each other in public or stop gazing intently into one another's eyes in front of cameras, it's too much. And we all know, too much of a good thing is, well, too much.

The media can give the public the big scoop on a couple's break up, but no one really knows what goes on behind closed doors. Couple's therapists may come close to knowing the facts as we hear the most private details from both spouses, but even we don't know what really happens, only that there are at least two sides to any story.

Television offers fantasy and entertainment in an attention deficit world. Celebrity divorces make for big juicy stories, complete with embellishments and paparazzi photos, all on a reality TV budget. Relationships and marriages exist in reality—his, hers, theirs, and everything in between. Photos involve the kids and the dog and the grandparents. Divorces are sad and disappointing and have to be squeezed in between cutting the grass and doing the laundry. Now, who would want to watch that story on the news?

Love and Life after Infidelity

Just as I was getting ready to write about infidelity, again, another major story is breaking news. No matter how many times we hear about it, regardless of the specific details, it is a subject that seems guaranteed to get strong reactions and no end of opinions.

Often couples choose to stay together after an infidelity has been discovered. Entering therapy is not about returning the marriage to its former state. Getting back to where they were previously in the relationship is not possible as circumstances have changed the dynamics forever. What is possible is to resurrect the attraction and build on any goodwill that remains. A common history and shared life carry a lot of weight in motivating a couple to work things out.

The goal of this type of couple's therapy is to create a new and improved marriage where trust is re-established, communication is strong, and intimacy is sacred. The work is hard, beyond hard. It is not quick and it is not short term, so finding the right therapist is a critical part of the recovery process. Going it alone without the help of a professional reduces the chances of success as best intentions alone are rarely enough to achieve the desired results.

Infidelity comes with some interesting cultural dynamics. It is a myth that men are the ones who cheat and women are the victims. Because women are suspected less, they may get away with it more, but women cheat, too. When husbands cheat, wives tend to blame themselves, head for the gym, lose weight, and buy sexy new clothes, in effect punishing the victim and rewarding the crime. Many husbands, on the other hand, lash out and blame the "other man," ready to go beat the daylights out of him. This may be satisfying in the short term but not very productive in healing the marriage, and misses the point all together. The anguish suffered by the injured party, however, is an equal opportunity tormentor, showing no mercy and no gender preference.

While each case and situation is unique to the particular couple, the recovery process does have some predictable patterns. First is dealing with crisis management following discovery. Usually both want to save the marriage or they wouldn't come to counseling, but emotions are so raw neither knows where to begin or what is even safe to say, let alone do. Start by fastening your seat belt because it is certain to be a bumpy ride.

Next comes assimilating and grieving this new information–the end of the marriage as it was and will not be again, as well as the lost innocence of believing this only happens to other people. It is common to roller coaster back and forth between a renewed infatuation between the spouses to full blown rage, sometimes from one hour to the next. How confusing when the person you always turned to for support in difficult times of your life is now the focus of the problem.

For those who make the commitment and persevere, next comes the challenging but rewarding proactive work of creating the new relationship. This is when couples learn and practice new communication skills, learn how to have healthy conflict, gain greater understanding of one another as individuals as well as spouses, and yes, may even have improved intimacy and better sex. The work of repairing and re-starting a marriage after infidelity asks a great deal of both partners with no guarantees of the outcome, but for many who are willing to take the risk the rewards can be greater than ever imagined.

Divorce Remorse

I am so sick of my partner that even the way he chews his food makes me nuts. I am so sick of my spouse that just hearing her voice grates on my nerves. I know he leaves the toilet seat up just to make me mad. I know she deliberately works late leaving me with the kids on nights I want to go out with my buddies. He thinks he knows everything. She is such a nag. I wish I was single again!

It's hard to believe that anyone who ends a relationship that looks and sounds like this could ever possibly regret the decision, but the reality is that many do. How could this be?

What we focus on is what grows. When we want or need to be angry or we simply are angry with our partner, we tend to focus on everything negative he or she does and quickly dismiss anything positive. The flip side of the same coin is when we are in a new romance. Our fresh love interest is perfect, our soul mate, and shares all our interests and desires. In the light of day, neither perspective is objective or real, regardless of how certain it may feel at the time. Consciously or unconsciously, positively or negatively, we work to prove ourselves right.

So, you get a divorce. Time goes by and emotions settle as you find your new routine, your New Normal. You and your ex have both moved on and created new lives for yourselves. You admit there are some things you really miss about your ex and about that relationship. You realize there are things that didn't turn out exactly as you'd imagined in your return to single life. The friends you wanted to be free to party with turned out to be not such good friends and the partying got old, fast. When you walk in after a long day to silence, you remember how you used to come home to a warm hug and maybe a meal to match. If there are children involved, having time to yourself may turn into too much time with yourself, and too little time with your children who you miss when they are with their other parent.

By the time the realization sets in and the emotions have shifted, and the ex starts looking pretty good again, the relationship is in the rear-view mirror. Some try reconciliation and a few even succeed, but most often too much damage has been done and repair is not an option. We find out too late, we had it all, or at least pretty good, and we didn't even know it.

The Silent Treatment—Passive Aggression

Passive-aggression is a term you hear often but may not know what it means. One thing is for sure, you know it isn't a compliment if someone says it about you. If it's something you encounter in another person in your life, you will instantly recognize how frustrating the behavior can be when it is directed at you--whether you know what it's called or not.

Passive-aggression refers to a way of behaving in a conflicted situation. By doing absolutely nothing in response to the other person, you are in complete control. If you are in a heated argument and walk out, or just refuse to say anything to avoid further interaction, you are behaving in a passive-aggressive manner. If you are not present, the argument stops by default. The other person is left in the position of waiting for you to return or participate in some way, knowing there is a risk you will simply withdraw again.

Engaging in passive-aggressive behaviors is never about conflict resolution. These types of interactions reflect an imbalance of power. In an effort to control the situation and the outcome, only one person's agenda matters.

Often people who behave in unhealthy ways don't even know they are doing it. It is possible to unknowingly cope in the way you learned as a child, not realizing it didn't work well then either. The unhealthy behavior can be reinforced by giving the appearance of shutting down conflict, when in reality the only thing shut down is communication.

Unlike passive-aggressive behavior, the goal of purely aggressive behavior is to force the other person into submission through words or actions or both. Removing yourself from this situation is wise but should always be done carefully, with all thoughts on safety.

If you find yourself withdrawing from interacting with your partner because you have reached a point of apathy, you are not behaving in a passive-aggressive way. This is not goal-directed behavior, rather it is resignation that change is no longer seen as a viable option for whatever reason. When a conflicted relationship involves an apathetic or disengaged partner, the relationship is in critical condition. This would be a good time to take a serious inventory to determine where you are and what you want your future to look like.

There are many healthy and productive ways to handle conflict in interactions with others, whether it's with spouses, friends, co-workers, or anyone in your life. Successful communication involves engaged people demonstrating respect for Self and others in a way that benefits both. Great communication doesn't happen by accident or without effort, and when it works well, it is a beautiful and satisfying thing.

The Texting Wars

I'm not going to go off on a tangent about how texting is destroying peoples' grammar and spelling skills, let alone ability to write an intelligent sentence. I'm not going to rag on my own kid who laughing said my opinion on the subject was because I am "old." And I won't talk about the dangers of texting and driving because we all know about that subject too well. What I will talk about is the fights I witness in my office over what I will boldly describe as obsessive texting.

I hate to do it, but I have to throw the ladies under the bus here. Ladies, you get so caught up in your phone and texting, you forget your husband, your boyfriend, your kids, your meal, even your surroundings. Ever wonder what you are missing? Ever wonder if it bothers your partner? It sure bothers many of the men I see in couples counseling.

In defense of the females, I'm as sure as I can be that it is the same part of the brain that makes women good at multitasking that also makes texting so enticing. Texting allows connection with multiple people in a very short period of time while also checking out dinner options, headline news, the weather, the movie schedule, buying the newest song and playing a favorite game—while never having to move from one place to another. As caught up as the ladies can be in what they are doing is as absent as they can be from the people in their physical presence.

I suspect by now the husbands and boyfriends are ready to read this out loud to their ladies, but I'd hold off if I were you. It's no secret most women need to feel connected, express their emotions, and demonstrate nurturing for others by reaching out in a caring manner. How many of you guys provide that emotional connection for your gals? Do you really listen? Do you try to fix her problems rather than pay attention to what she is trying to tell you? Could you describe the feelings she just shared? Do you pretend to listen while checking the game score on your own phone? You may laugh, but is it really funny? Is it really that different?

It doesn't have to be as bleak as it might appear. Some simple efforts can yield quick and positive results. Consider setting no-texting times each day. Agree with your partner to take turns talking while the other just listens, without interruption. Make a coffee date like when you first met and leave the phones in the car for a whole hour. You'll be okay, I promise. Commit to making and sustaining even just a few small changes and hopefully your relationship will be alive and well long after texting is gone, and has been replaced with the next new high tech toy.

Loneliness

Discussions about feelings of loneliness have been one of the most persistently talked about and lamented subjects in my practice. Even those who say they are comfortable being alone will say they are anything but comfortable with being lonely. Is it the human condition? How did we all get so disconnected?

Many single people begrudge their solo status believing that finding the right partner will end their unhappiness. Some married people will tell you they are more alone in their relationships than they ever were when they were single and envy those who are. There are people who believe that not having children has left them suffering loneliness in their mid years and after, while others will say their adult children have made their lives beyond difficult. The "good old days" when generations of families all lived on the same block or even in the same house may have been good for some but quite the opposite for others. It seems there are no guarantees against loneliness simply based on relationship status. Those waiting for a change as the cure may find themselves even more disappointed when reality does not match fantasy.

I was in a meeting recently and was observing behaviors of the people present. There was a speaker, two people obviously listening, and the rest were on their phones texting. Forget about this being rude, and it is, but we've lost ourselves in the age of technology. How can anyone wonder why we are so isolated? Add that many of us work too much and play is often done in loud places with bodies crammed together, no quality conversation possible, and it can't be any wonder we are feeling so lonely.

A woman told me once she was in such need of male attention and affection that she was considering hiring a male prostitute. I asked her, "If your goal is to not feel lonely, then how will you feel when the man leaves with the money you paid and you are standing at the door alone?" She thought for a moment and then quickly dismissed the idea. Quick fixes don't often prove to be good fixes.

Until that special person shows up, be willing to sit with your discomfort knowing it can and will change. Be realistic but challenge yourself to get out of your comfort zone, which may be part of the problem. Determine behaviors you want to eliminate that have left you more disconnected instead of less. Make a list of new things you are willing to try or try again. Learn to enjoy your own company by doing things on your own. Be honest with yourself that if you are home every evening in your sweats, eating dinner in front of the TV and going to bed early, you aren't really looking for a relationship right now, and that can be a viable option, too.

Dating 101

It doesn't matter how old you are or what you do for a living, if you don't want to depend on Fate to present you with your soul mate, you are probably going to find yourself in the world of dating. Are you sick of hearing from well-intentioned coupled friends and family that the perfect person for you is just around the corner? Have you given up on meeting the love of your life at the gym? Maybe it's time to take control of your own social life.

The first step is to figure out where you want to go to meet like-minded people. If there is a sport you enjoy, that might be a good option for meeting other singles who like the same activity. If you have strong political leanings, getting involved in a campaign could be the place to go. Options are only limited by your preferences and time available. Choosing activities you enjoy ensures you will have a good time, no matter what, and people having a good time are more attractive than people who aren't.

Whether you meet people online, at speed dating events, at organized singles mixers, by matchmaking friends and family, or anywhere else you can think of, it's good to remember that the odds are not in favor of the first one being The One. Keep an open mind and don't give up.

The dating process is a good way to learn about what you do and don't want in a potential partner, as well as how you present yourself to others. If you like someone but that person isn't interested in you, it only means you don't match what the other person is looking to find. If you meet someone who likes you but you don't feel the same, that person doesn't match what you are hoping to find. It isn't personal and it really can be that simple. And bad dates always make fun dinner conversations with friends later, so all is not lost if things don't go well.

It is good to have some basic rules in mind before and as you go through your dating experience. Here are a few of the tried and true tips from my practice where relationships are the major focus of daily discussions.

- ❧ The ONLY goal of a first date is to decide if there is going to be a second date! Keep it light, keep it fun, and keep it short.
- ❧ Listen more than you talk. Your goal is to learn about the new person and that means hearing what they are saying.
- ❧ Give the person a chance. While it's true that first impressions count, most people are nervous on first dates and may need a little time to relax.
- ❧ If and when you get frustrated, take a break and start over later. If you force yourself to keep dating when your enthusiasm has dwindled, you are not likely going to present yourself at your best or be completely open to the experience.
- ❧ Tell the truth. Lying about your age, your marital status, whether you have children can really backfire, especially if you like the person and later have to explain how your first interactions included you misrepresenting yourself.
- ❧ If you meet someone you really do like and the feeling is mutual, remember that our brains during infatuation make us silly in ways we may regret later. Enjoy the feeling and the fun, but avoid making major decisions until your feet are back on solid ground.

Dinner for One

You walk into a restaurant, looking forward to a nice meal, maybe a chance to read your book or just sit back and relax after a hectic day. You smile as the host approaches until you are asked, "Just one?"

Being single has finally come into its own as a valid life option, yet the world continues to favor and validate couples. From laws to taxes to social settings to health insurance, being single has always taken a distant second to going the marriage route. More than questionable and grossly oversimplified statistics report that married people are healthier than single people. Entire books have been written by recognized and respected experts claiming we are not whole until we live our lives in a committed marital relationship.

Perhaps it's true that nothing challenges our personal growth more than a romantic relationship where we have so much to gain and so much to lose. However, to diminish unattached adults with such a generic and sweeping claim fails to recognize the uniqueness of each individual, and the complex diversity of an array of relationships. For some, marriage comes easily while a relationship with a parent or sibling or child exasperates the best of intentions and efforts. For others, marriage may be the result of a poor choice that only represents a problem to be solved while other relationships may be healthy and fulfilling. Complications and challenges in all combinations of relationships are the daily subjects of many if not most family therapy sessions. All have their challenges, and all have their lessons to be learned.

Most of us would agree that life with a great relationship is nicer than one without. But, what if you aren't in a relationship? The theory in question is that you can never realize your full potential if you remain single and unattached. Well, you will also never reach your full educational potential if you don't get a Ph.D. You will never reach your full physical potential if you don't run marathons. And, if you never have the experience of learning to live a happy and healthy life as a single person, you will never know what your full potential as an independent individual might have been.

Until that great relationship appears, and if it doesn't, take yourself out to dinner. Take your book you are looking forward to reading. Savor perusing the menu to choose the fabulous dish you want to eat for your relaxing dinner. Make no apologies for being solo and enjoy your own company. The next time you are asked, answer with confidence, "No, not 'just one,' one!"

Family & Parenting

Good Dads Make Healthy Daughters

While little girls watch their mothers closely as their role models, they look to their fathers for their sense of self-worth. The messages the daughter receives from the father, from overt to implied, have a major impact on the girl's developing self-esteem.

When considering the impact of a father's presence, it is important to consider the daughter's age and developmental stage. The greatest impact I have seen repeatedly and consistently in my practice has been roughly between the ages of 5 and 8. Trying to logically figure out how a little girl this age is affected using adult thinking can be a guarantee of getting it wrong. To understand the impact requires the use of child logic. For example, a girl who feels her father does not love or want her believes there is something wrong with her, instead of there being something wrong with her father, the man she sees as larger than life.

An absent father during early formative years can be the cause of what is often referred to as an "abandonment script." There are many different ways a father can be absent and abandon his child. A father in the room who is passed out drunk on the sofa is absent. A father who abuses his child or his family verbally, emotionally, physically is absent as a father but present as a bully. A young girl who is abandoned by her father is programmed to seek the attention and approval of male figures, never feeling good enough and sabotaging herself by the very choices she makes. These girls grow up to be women who may set themselves up to unknowingly repeat the abandonment they know and subconsciously believe they deserve.

Conversely, I have seen the positive results of good parenting by some great fathers. I have seen divorced fathers, fathers who work long hours, military fathers away for long periods all have a very affirming presence in their daughter's lives. Modern day inventions have made staying in touch easier than ever, and new trends in co-parenting for divorced parents who succeed in putting their children first can pay off big time. A father who ensures his loving words and actions are in sync and delivers the consistent message to his young daughter that he cares and can be counted on is an important investment into the daughter's mental health and long-term happiness. Dads matter and they matter a lot.

What is an Identified Patient?

The concept of the "identified patient" (IP) is an old and accepted one in the world of mental health. It originated decades ago as the result of a study done in an inpatient mental health facility with patients who were improving and ready to leave the hospital setting. Half were sent back to their homes, to what we call their "families of origin," and the patients relapsed. The other half were moved to a professionally supervised step-down program and succeeded in rejoining mainstream society. Surprisingly, in the second group that thrived, someone else back in their families of origin got sick—the new IP. This shifted the focus from an isolated individual to seeing the patient as part of a family and community system, the beginning of family therapy and the family systems model of treatment.

Often members of these families have no awareness of their dysfunction, partially because they are so focused on the IP as the problem. Also, the pathology may be multi-generational disguising abnormal and unhealthy behaviors as normal, when in fact all they really are is familiar. Problems typically develop when the child enters young adulthood and begins to resist the undesirable role in the family for the first time. Any outsider attempting to enter the system to help, like a physician or school counselor or therapist, will almost certainly be met with hostility as they represent a threat to the family's well-entrenched status quo.

How can you determine if you might be the IP for your family of origin? The short answer is to look for goal-oriented control and sabotage. This type of family system pushes to control every decision, every option for the IP with the intent of keeping the IP solidly in this role, including and especially believing there is no other option. They may control your friends and relationships, your social activities and hobbies, the job you do or don't take, where you go to college or even if you go to college at all. They may decide when and if you move out on your own and where you will live when you do. They will attempt to control your very Self, your image of who you are by constantly telling you who you are.

If control doesn't work and the IP dares to branch out solo in pursuit of dreams and desires—a healthy and normal choice for any young person, expect sabotage. Sabotage comes in many forms, from subtle to deafening. Maybe they agree to pay for college if you go down the street but not if you go away, even if away costs less and offers a better education. They may start out paying for you to go to therapy but withdraw funds and approval when they see changes beginning to happen, especially if those changes involve you thinking independently and differently. Maybe you introduce your new significant other to the family and that person is treated in a way that sends them running for the hills--and out of your life. Look for shaming messages that always end in the same place— there is something wrong with YOU and THEY are the solution.

It takes a lot of courage and strength for the IP to stand up and declare, "No more!" The path is never a short or easy one, but the rewards can be so worth it. Imagine finding your voice, your passions, your happiness, your Self. Imagine living your life to the fullest and on your own terms.

How to Win at Parenting Your Teenager

As parents of young children, our job first and foremost is to protect our babies and keep them safe. Whether it is testing formula on our wrist, putting a gate in front of a step or training wheels on a new bicycle, we are ever vigilant to the dangers of the world around us.

As those children grow and change, seemingly in the blink of an eye, so does our job as a parent. It's now time to teach our budding adults good decision making skills and give them every possible opportunity to practice. Our kids need to know how to think independently so that when they are out and unsupervised, they make healthy and confident choices. Should I try the drugs others are using so I can be accepted? Is it a big deal to get in a car with a driver who has been drinking? What should I do about sex?

Instead of telling your teen what to do, ask, "What are you going to do?" I was told about a teen that had planned a magical date for a big school dance and just assumed the parents would pay what would inevitably be a whopper of a price tag. Instead of a scolding or flat out denial, I encouraged affirming the child and then getting curious. "That's really creative and sounds like a lot of fun, honey. Have you checked into prices so you know how much you can afford?" The teen proceeded to get on the internet to research prices and quickly decided to pass on the limo, asking Dad if he would be the driver instead. What a great opportunity to start teaching budgeting and planning, and for parents to relax with dad publically playing chauffeur but secretly being the chaperone.

Handle all subjects as a priority, and if the timing is poor make sure you follow up later. Even if you feel the subject is insignificant, don't dismiss what your teen is sharing. I remember curling up on my mom's bed one night when I was very young and asking her what it felt like to fall in love. Of course I thought I already had and of course she knew that. She listened patiently, never made fun, and offered a few words of comfort. I went to bed happy and feeling safe knowing I could always go back to my mom, no matter what. Being available for small things now is the path to being a resource for the big things later.

Last, unless asked (and you won't be), don't start telling your teen what it was like when you were a kid, or even worse, that it was the same for you as it is for your teen today. It isn't the same and instantly shuts down the discussion from being about the teen to being all about the parent. Ask your child what it's like to be a teen today on any subject rather than assuming you know. Use follow-up questions to increase your understanding and show you are listening. You might just be surprised at what you hear.

Special Parents Raising Special Kids

I have come to know, both personally and professionally, an increasing number of parents who are raising kids with special needs. In fact, I was and am one of those parents and now grandparents. We are an elite group, surely with reserved seating in heaven. Maybe the only thing more challenging than raising them is resisting how precious and adorable and bright and funny they can be.

I remember one parent telling me, "It's just too hard. I can't do it." I simply asked her, "Is quitting an option?" For the vast majority of us, it isn't. The truth is we don't want to quit, we just want it to get easier so we can enjoy our children and our children can enjoy being kids. We want our relationship to be with our child, no matter what age, and not the diagnosis we face as a family.

There are so many great moms and dads who do amazing jobs of taking care of their kids' needs. With endless hope, they take them to therapy and doctors appointments. They work with them at home on behavior, motor skills and speech. They read voraciously, trying to gain some sense of success through knowledge. They make special foods and manage special diets, knowing efforts may end in frustration when the child refuses to cooperate. And they collapse into bed each night acknowledging to themselves they have to get up and do it all again tomorrow.

What is missing from this picture? It is something so obvious yet it seems to be the last thing on the list, if it is even on the list at all. Shame on the experts who ignore it! Woe to the couples who neglect it. That key critical element is the parents' relationship--the foundation for the family and the team that keeps it all going. No treatment plan that excludes this piece of the puzzle can be complete. Romance left to spontaneity too often gets trumped by fatigue and intimacy dwindles, perhaps going without notice until the marriage is at risk or worse.

Couples time does not have to demand a huge chunk out of an already full schedule, making it just one more thing on the to-do list. It can be as simple as a short coffee date where you talk about anything but the kids. It can be something as seemingly un-romantic as marriage counseling, devoting one hour out of an entire week to focus on your relationship in an adults-only setting.

Plan a date now, and another and another after that. Make a treatment plan for your marriage that allows you to be each other's safe place for the best and the worst of times, and everything in between. If you think it's hard doing it together, think about doing it alone.

The Ultimate Parenting Challenge

What is the absolute most difficult part of being a parent? What do you think? Is it getting up in the middle of the night when you are exhausted to attend to a hungry baby or frightened child? Is it getting the little darlings into bed at night against unending protests and desperate pleas for another drink of water? Is it getting them to clean up their rooms or do their homework or eat their vegetables?

The absolute most difficult part of being a parent is seeing your child hurt, knowing you can't do anything to make it stop. I don't care if you are the parent of a young child who just scored the final out of the championship game, or if you are sitting with your adult child who is grieving the end of a romance, it hurts to watch your child hurt. Always. Forever. Completely.

The thing about difficult life experiences is they are often the best lessons for all of us. I don't know who came up with this system, but I sure wouldn't have voted for it. I do know as I look back over my own life, some of the darkest moments and days have been the most significant learning and character building events in helping me become the person I am today. It begs the question, if we could protect our children from ever experiencing painful disappointments, should we?

It can be a fine line between helping our children by providing some type of intervention and helping our children by being there to offer support as they have their own life experiences. Obviously the decision of which is best will always be on a case-by-case basis, but a good guide to follow is to avoid telling your child what to do with challenges. Unsolicited advice is not often helpful or welcome, but being invited by your child into his or her world during the most difficult times can be golden.

Parents and Children as Best Friends

As the world continues to lose incredibly talented performers to too many drug overdoses, we hear repeated stories of a parent and child who were "best friends." It's easy to understand how a life of fame lived on the road could easily create this dynamic, but is it ever a good idea for parents and children to be best friends? Is it even possible?

A healthy relationship between friends, by its very definition, is a relationship between equals. This is the great power of a best friend—we can both be ourselves with unconditional acceptance and without judgment. This is where we have the luxury of feeling truly safe.

A parent-child relationship by its nature is a one-up-one-down relationship, not equal. The parent is the caregiver from the start, the provider, the teacher, the guide, the permission giver, the disciplinarian and the problem solver, always responsible for the child.

The idea that an addicted parent and his or her child could be "best friends" is misleading, at best. A parent, whose primary relationship is with drugs or alcohol unfairly puts the child in the role of caregiver, grown up way too soon in a toxic environment destined to result in a missed childhood with too many scars left behind.

The ideal best friend for a child is another child, leaving parents to function in the most important role of all. Friends may come and friends may go over the course of a lifetime, but you only get one original Mom and one original Dad, both in a special category all by themselves.

Attached or Detached Parenting

You may or may not be familiar with the term "Attachment Parenting," but you have likely been exposed to debates about it through recurring stories in the media. Maybe you are considering doing it yourself.

Proponents sleep with their babies, seldom lay them down but always pick them up when they cry, and breastfeed possibly for years. They argue that this is the best way to parent with less constituting possible child abandonment. Opponents of the theory feel that it is developmentally important for babies to learn to soothe and calm themselves when they are agitated, and that it is dangerous to have a small infant sleep in an adult bed with big adult bodies. They argue that this theory and the related behaviors are extreme, unhealthy and poorly validated.

Breastfeeding is often used as the main point of debate, as if breastfeeding--a healthy human process--is linked with the theory of "Attachment Parenting"--a recent concept developed by a pediatrician. Putting the two subjects together is misleading, at best, but doing so certainly makes the stories much more provocative for the cover of magazines. Obviously, not all mothers who breastfeed are practicing "Attachment Parenting" and parents who choose to bottle feed their babies are not practicing detachment parenting.

The well-being of the relationships of individuals, couples and families throughout the life cycle is the focus of the counseling work of Marriage and Family Therapists. I have encountered "Attachment Parenting" multiple times in my practice, and I have to say it does not look like the stories I have seen portrayed on television or in magazines.

Where are the couples? Where are the husbands, the fathers? Where are the families? Images are consistently focused on the mother and the "attached" child. I have worked with couples who were practicing "Attachment Parenting" where the intimacy of their relationships had broken down and the marriages were at serious risk. Husbands and new fathers said they felt left out. They struggled to bond with their own babies, said they did not feel connected to their wives and some questioned whether they would be receptive to ever having more children. Grandparents described being confused, wanting to participate and support the young parents but not knowing how or where they fit in.

If you are exploring different theories of parenting to decide what is best for you and your young family:

- Research each option thoroughly. Pay attention to what both proponents and opponents have to say.
- Check to see if someone selling their name, idea, or book may also be selling products for profit. Are you buying a concept, or are you buying into a marketing campaign?
- Seek input from your obstetrician, your pediatrician, a pediatric nurse, a Marriage and Family Therapist and anyone else you believe is a credible resource. Don't forget to ask your parents and grandparents because the world may have changed since they had new families, but the basic needs of babies remain pretty much the same.
- Be careful not to get so caught up in the research and all the expert opinions that you can't hear the real expert in the house right there with you, the one who is making it very clear a diaper change is in order.

- Think about whether you have said or heard others complain their mothers held them too much or too little. I have never seen this as a presenting issue in therapy, however, I regularly see people coping with problems resulting from parents who have remained too attached for too long. The discussion about healthy attachment is incomplete without considering the entire family and changes that naturally occur throughout the life span.
- Relax and pace yourself because as soon as you master understanding and meeting your baby's current needs, your child will change and grow and that will demand that you change and grow as a parent just to try and keep up.

The Worst Question You Can Ask Your ADHD Kid

Why did you DO that?!

It isn't that they don't know the answer. It isn't that they just aren't very bright. It is that they know how you will react if they tell you the truth. "Because I wanted to."

Wow. If you weren't frustrated enough already, what would that answer do to your blood pressure? Maybe hearing, "I don't know, " or a pre-emptive, "I'm sorry," really is a better choice of response for the poor kid who knows all too well how it feels to be between a rock and a hard place.

What's the solution? First, don't ask WHY questions? Second, acknowledge to yourself you already know the answer to the question you wish you hadn't asked. Third, work with your child to help him or her to think about behavior and consequence. Last, if you blow it and the WHY question comes out of your mouth before you can stop, give yourself a break. Maybe your truth about why you asked is "BECAUSE I WANTED TO!"

Staying Together for the Children

If you want to do what is best for your children, fix your marriage. If you cannot fix your marriage, do what is best for your children.

Who hasn't heard someone say they are committed to a bad marriage because they are "staying together for the sake of the children?" Maybe the intentions are the absolute best, or maybe it's a cover for fear of having to start over, maybe it's a lot of things. What it can never be is what is best for the children.

Reports pop up in the media from time to time that support one position or another but they typically are funded by special interest groups, conducted by those with an agenda to prove their own point. Results of research may be reported superficially without all the details disclosed, distorting the reported information. It doesn't take research to know that what is ideal for children and parents is to have two happy, healthy, loving adults raising children in a peaceful home. Unfortunately for many, sometimes that is just not the case.

Keeping a relationship together for the children makes the children the reason for the marriage, in effect making the kids responsible for the adults' relationship. I recall a young adult talking to me about foregoing an amazing out-of-state educational opportunity because she felt she was the glue holding her parents together. She ended up deciding to take the opportunity and her parents were divorced shortly after, suggesting a distorted cause and effect for the adult child who was never responsible for the parent's marriage, let alone their divorce.

As parents, we are the role models for our children, constantly teaching what marriage and relationships look like—good or bad. What are you teaching your children? Do you hope they will grow up and have the marriage you have today? If the answer is yes, pat yourself on the back repeatedly and keep up the good work. If the answer is no, it's never too late to make healthy course corrections, whether the decision is to stay together or to move apart. Marriage counseling can help.

Contracting for Successful Co-Parenting

When shared custody began to be the norm for divorcing couples with minor children, many of us family therapists met the idea with disdain and skepticism. If a couple could not get along well enough to stay married, why would the courts think they could get along well enough to raise children together? Now, years later, many have shown it can work and work well. When parents are able to commit to putting the needs of their children first over their own emotions, the children benefit, and when children benefit the parents benefit.

There is a tendency for parents to focus on the age of the children at the time of divorce when setting up co-parenting plans. Short-sighted thinking makes plans obsolete as fast as the children can age, and may leave the door open for future conflict even in the best of situations. In time the parents inevitably move on as well, creating new lives, new homes, new relationships, and a plethora of changes that are often unpredictable.

Even the best of co-parented divorced families can face challenges when a new person enters the picture with his or her own values, opinions, beliefs, traditions, and of course, family. Creating a healthy "blended family" where each is honored and respected, and ultimately integrated, requires compromise and time to evolve. Avoiding pitfalls early on can be a smart way to begin.

Creating a Co-Parenting Contract takes co-parenting agreements to a whole new level. This type of contract would not be legally binding but would clearly lay out the intent of both parents as to how they mutually agree they want to go forward. It would be written out, signed and dated, and each would maintain a copy. It is negotiated by the parents as the authority figures and without the involvement of the children. Conditions for amendments to the document would ideally be described to allow for flexibility along the way. Having this contract in place from the start can also be helpful to a new person later entering the existing family system to help avoid pitfalls that can damage a new and growing relationship.

Consider the following questions as a place to start.

- When is it appropriate to introduce the children to someone new that a parent is dating? Who will tell them and how? The same question applies to announcing an engagement and new marriage.
- What is okay or not okay to call a step-parent or step-grandparents? Answers vary from one case to another, but left to chance can wreak havoc. Leaving children to decide what they will call a new person in the family puts an adult decision unfairly on young shoulders, and should not be compared to a baby creating a pet name for a grandparent.
- How can you minimize your kids playing one parent off the other? Kids manipulate and kids challenge, taking it to an Olympic level when teen years arrive. How do you plan to keep the adults in charge and the kids as kids? What is the best way to be proactive instead of reactive when challenges arise?
- How would you like to address inevitable conflicts that will develop over time when unanticipated events occur? Do you want to solicit the help of grandparents who may be more objectively focused on the well-being of the

children? Do you want to agree proactively that mother and father will seek the assistance of a qualified family therapist? What other options do you want to consider?

❧ What is important for you to have on your list so that you feel confident committing to and signing your agreement? Is the agreement one you could comfortably show to your future fiancé so that he or she would understand how best to support you in your role as a parent?

Divorce under the best of circumstances is never easy. Co-parenting children after divorce is even harder. Creating healthy blended families may be the most difficult challenge of all. Success is available for those who know what matters most and are willing to go the distance to achieve it.

The Paradox of Time

I was in the fifth grade when I found my absolute favorite book in the Children's Library. It was Madeleine L'Engle's fantasy story, *A Wrinkle in Time*. What first attracted me to the book was a big, gold seal on the cover that indicated the book was the winner of the Newbery Gold Medal Award. To be honest, I had no earthly clue what that was or what it meant, but it sure was impressive, and the book went home with me. I immediately started to read and I did not put the book back down until I finished the last page.

Then there was a wrinkle in my own time. I read this wonderful book again, only this time I was a mother reading it to my own children. I read aloud the familiar words and watched the delight on my young sons' faces as they experienced this wonderful story for the first time. But, there was something unsettling to me in the experience, even a little confusing. How, in the blink of an eye, did I become the mother instead of the child?

Then there was another wrinkle. A giant wrinkle! Two of my grandkids are with me for a sleepover. They seem to have an endless supply of energy and find it difficult to cohabitate the same room for more than five minutes without needing a referee—some things about raising boys never change. But last night at bedtime, magic happened. I began reading the book to them. They both crawled up in the chair with me, along with one of the dogs, and no the chair is not that big. They were glued to learning about Meg and

Charles Wallace, Mrs. Whatsit, Mrs. Who, Mrs. Which and teased into wondering exactly what a time tesseract might be. I remember the feeling.

How strange that so much time has passed with so much the same yet at the same time so different. The wonderful book is just as wonderful. Children are enjoying it as much today as they did decades ago. I'm still here and I still love *A Wrinkle in Time*, but I am no longer the young girl lost in the library or the young mother tucking her babies into bed at night. Last night, instead of reading to my grandchildren from a book I held in my hands as I turned the pages, I read to them from an eBook and clicked on the screen to turn the pages. I wonder what the next wrinkle in time has in store for me, and I wonder what Madeleine L'Engle would have to say about people reading her book on their handheld computer devices.

Holiday Stress

I swear I didn't really want to write on this topic, but an annoying voice in my ear forced me to do it. I'm pretty sure it's the same one that is nagging me in my waking and sleeping hours right now. "There's so much to do, you don't have time to rest! You already waited too long and will have to stand in line forever at the post office. What do you mean you aren't baking cookies? You didn't put up a tree!"

When I try to identify the voice, it does sound familiar. It's definitely female with a determined agenda. Could it be my mother who worked so hard as a single mom to make the holidays special for her children? Is it my grandmother who surprised each and every one of her grandkids with something special every year? Is it my aunt who decorates her house so beautifully it puts Macy's to shame? Maybe.... But wait, I think I know. It sounds very familiar. It's me!

Why on earth do we do this to ourselves? Why do we spend money we can't afford, eat food we shouldn't eat and commit to more events than there are days in the week? You could argue that the reason is because it's a religious holiday, but I don't buy it. Many people who are not religious or are not Christian go through the same dance. How did something that used to be so much fun turn into retailers putting out the merchandise before Halloween and crowds the day after Thanksgiving needing to be kept in check by Security Swat Teams? Dare I say it? It's CRAZY!

Now, this is the point in my writings where I try to offer something constructive, encouraging and make suggestions that might be helpful. I'm sorry to say it, but I'm afraid I am going fail in meeting that goal this time. I have more shopping to do. There are presents to wrap. I have to figure out what I'm cooking for Christmas dinner, make my grocery list and get to the store to buy all the ingredients. I hope I don't forget something and have to go back out. What if I don't have enough gift wrap to finish the presents? How much should I tip my bug guy and do I have to put it in a card? HO HO HO, indeed.

Santa's Naughty List

I think one of the best parts of the holiday season is remembering favorite stories of years gone by. I thought it might be fun to share one of my own that has well withstood the test of time as I am still laughing as I tell you about it today. Maybe it's just me, maybe you had to be there, but I bet you will laugh, too.

I was in the seventh grade when we used to call it Junior High School. The preacher's kid from the church we attended was transferred into my class, and Jeff and I became quick friends. I regularly looked forward to Monday mornings when he would quietly fill me in on all the juicy congregation gossip from the previous week, all the stuff they didn't talk about on Sunday mornings.

It was Christmas and time for Jeff to give me the inside scoop on the party the prior weekend at his house. He described to me how the soloist from the church choir drank too much and actually stood on a table with a lampshade on her head as she belted out a song. It didn't help matters that it was a widely shared opinion that this woman, soloist or not, couldn't carry a tune to save her soul.

We went to church the following Sunday for the holiday service. Lined up in the pew was my mom, my younger brother, me in the middle, my best friend, Cyndy, and finally my older brother at the end. We took up most of the row with our holiday-adorned presence as well as our good intentions.

The service started out as expected but took a precarious turn when the minister stood up and gave a glowing introduction for the soloist as she came forward to perform her Christmas number. I never told anyone what Jeff had shared with me in confidence, but my loyal silence came with a price.

The woman began to sing and proceeded to hit her usual sour notes at random points in her solo. When she finished, you could hear a pin drop until the minister stood up, looked somberly at the congregation and rhetorically asked, "Now wasn't that beautiful?" That's when I lost my battle for control as a loud snort escaped and I burst into uncontrollable giggles. With no idea why I was laughing, Cyndy couldn't help herself and she joined in.

My mom looked down the row at me with that Mom Look, you know the one, admonishing me for my bad behavior without needing to say a word. I knew I was in trouble, but I couldn't help it. Mom's look only made me laugh harder. Next, my younger brother joined in and oh what a scene we must have made. The fact the others didn't even know why we were laughing made the situation, literally, hysterical.

Confused as to what was happening, my older brother leaned forward looking down the row at me as if to ask what he was missing that could possibly be so funny. Not understanding didn't stop him, and next he started laughing. To say I made a fool of myself would be a gross understatement. To say I did it alone would be a lie.

We all tried to pull ourselves together, we really did. No one looked at anyone else, and all eyes were straight forward as we each held our breath in a feeble attempt to regain control. We might have even been making some progress, until the final event sealed all our fates.

There was an older man sitting in the row directly behind us no one had paid any attention to, at least not until he ripped out a snore loud enough it could surely be heard at the North Pole. That was it. We all disintegrated into fits, including Mom who then started laughing, too.

I don't remember how we managed to escape, but I do know it was before the end of the service. I will never understand how the man behind us could have slept through our shenanigans, and surely some of this is his fault, too.

So, that's the story of how I got on Santa's Naughty List. You could argue whether it was worth it or not, but the damage is done and the price has to be paid. If you laughed, or even just cracked a smile at any point while reading this story, then you're on the List now, too.

The Power of Rituals

New Year's is a perfect time and holiday to talk about the power rituals can have in our lives. New Year's begs us to contemplate events of the past year while anticipating and celebrating the hope of the pristine New Year ahead. We have fireworks, toasts at midnight, a huge disco ball falling every year in Time Square, parties, special foods, to name just a few of the traditions.

When I grew up in Ohio, a New Year always began with the traditional meal of pork and sauerkraut. The smell of the kraut wafted through the house, permeating every nook and cranny, determined to chase away any lingering bad spirits. Now, sauerkraut is one of those dishes people either love or hate, so it could have been a good or bad thing to have that smell everywhere. Fortunately for me, I love sauerkraut.

I'll never forget the first New Year when my young children and I moved from Ohio to Atlanta, Georgia. I went to the grocery store in search of the ingredients for our annual New Year's dinner, the first in our new home that most certainly needed a Sauerkraut Ritual. Only I found none of the customary displays of ingredients or anything that looked familiar in any of the stores I visited. Baffled, I finally had to start asking, "Where is your supply of pork and sauerkraut for New Year's?" No one knew what I was talking about! I felt like I'd slipped through Alice's looking glass. Finally, I realized I was asking the wrong question. "What is the traditional

New Year's dinner here in the South?" The answer came quickly and consistently, "Black-eyed peas and ham hocks, of course!" Pigs feet? Gross! No sauerkraut? You're kidding, right?

This experience got me to think for the first time about how rituals can differ culturally and geographically and throughout time. Living in one place for the first 30 years of my life lulled me into the arrogance of thinking everyone else was like me, like us, the people who did it the right way, the way everyone else should do it. Today, many life experiences and locations later, I have come to honor the diversity and the significance of these rituals that in many ways define who we are as people.

Certainly it would be impossible to count or name all of the rituals practiced by as many people and cultures as exist and have existed on the planet. The rituals can be good, bad and everything in between. They can be simple like brushing our teeth every day, compulsive like washing hands repeatedly, cherished like birthdays, and complex like honoring the anniversary of Pearl Harbor. New Year's is a good time of year to think about the rituals you honor in your own life and why they are important to you. As for me, I'm making sauerkraut.

Good Therapy

Why Does Therapy Work?

Multiple things make therapy work, and there is ample research to prove it. Studies consistently find a positive relationship with the therapist is the first step to achieving favorable outcomes. Having a safe place to simply be vulnerable without judgment or restriction can provide a powerful release. Being able to speak freely without interruption or fear of hurting another person's feelings offers space to think and plan more clearly. These important things and more contribute to the positive outcome of therapy but are not what I believe is the most significant element.

If you are unaware of choices you may have available, then the choices are not available to you. If you try to do your absolute best with the purest of intentions but use the same skills you used before, you are likely to get disappointing results. Bringing a trained therapist into the process offers new perspectives and real possibility of productive results.

A therapist listens first to gain understanding of your particular situation and needs. Next we ask strategic questions designed to provoke fresh thinking about old dynamics. Finally, we offer psycho-educational tools designed to create new choices in thoughts and behaviors. For example, when someone comes in to see me after having an upsetting argument, we will review the events and surrounding emotions first. We might then re-process the interaction in a role play format in order to model and practice different ways of saying and handling the same situation but with improved results.

If you need someone to work on your plumbing, you call a plumber. If you need someone to work on your car, you call a mechanic. If you need someone to work on your mental health and happiness, call a therapist.

Buyer Beware!

No one calls a therapist for fun or when things are going well. Often people tell me they have had my number or website saved for months before they make that first important contact. With so many different licenses and certificates, degrees and programs, knowing what you are even looking for can be incredibly confusing.

A large family-owned business was knee deep in battle. Out of desperation and upon the recommendation of a friend, they hired a man who called himself an "interventionist," and they agreed to pay him a large lump sum of money for his services. When things in the family did not improve but in fact got worse, one family member chose individual counseling instead. Upon investigating the man's credentials it didn't take long to realize he didn't have any.

If you are considering inviting a mental health professional into your life, into your relationship, into your family, DO YOUR HOME-WORK FIRST. Once you are clear what your particular needs and goals are, start looking for the right services and the right provider for you.

Best Friends Are Not Therapists

Someone has said, and it is often repeated, that if you have a best friend you don't need a therapist. That person clearly didn't know the difference between the two.

I recently saw a car sticker that made me chuckle with its description of a best friend. "A friend will calm you down when you are angry, but a best friend will skip beside you with a baseball bat singing, 'Someone's gonna get it.'" Now, as a licensed professional, I have to acknowledge this is supposed to be funny and that I am not encouraging violence on behalf of friendship. I do know, however, I would never give up my best friend for all the tea in China--and I do love my tea.

A therapist is not and should not be a friend—ethically or legally. The therapist should be friendly, but being a friend is not our job or our role. The reverse is also true and echoes in my head from graduate school, "You cannot be a therapist to your own friends and family."

The job of a therapist is to always listen carefully, be relatively objective, and apply well-honed professional skills appropriately. A therapist helps you see options and choices in your life you may not have considered on your own. If this is not what you are getting from your therapist, ask for it. If you still don't get it, look for a new therapist. Bad therapy can be a complete waste of time and money, and worse, it can be harmful. Good therapy can change your world. Don't settle for less.

Career & Society

Mentors and Why You Want One

Being a mentor for a young person can be a very rewarding experience for both the mentor and the mentee. No one can say how much of the success of young professionals occurs because of the mentoring they receive, or how much is because successful people find good mentors as part of their overall plan. Regardless, having a good mentor is truly an invaluable asset.

I'll never forget the day early in my first career when I met the man who became my mentor, my guide, and ultimately my very dear friend. I was young and naïve but full of determination with no clue what a mentor was, let alone what a good one can do for you. I was lucky because my mentor found me. He helped me navigate my way through the giant and complex Fortune 500 world. He showed his own courage by knocking down walls to my benefit at a time when women in management were few and far between. He believed in me before I believed in myself.

Now, this is the point in my story when some people have said to me, "He was hitting on you." Nothing could be further from the truth. A good mentor, a real mentor knows the power he or she holds and would never use that to take advantage of the person they are helping. Those of us who found our own successes acknowledge none of us did it alone, and many feel an obligation to help others in the way we have been helped.

My relationship with my mentor changed over time into a lifelong friendship that included both our families, our dogs, eventually our experiences of becoming self employed, and his death a few years ago broke my heart. Without the help of my mentor, I never would have realized my own potential nor would I have had the career success I was able to achieve. He knew how grateful I was, but he could never know just how much.

Today there are many different types of mentoring programs. There are formal and informal programs in many if not most companies, big and small, as well as in schools and professional organizations. These are programs where someone is assigned to be a mentor, or a "buddy," to an incoming individual to help them meet people and learn how to navigate a new environment. I am a big supporter of these types of programs, but they are not the kind of mentoring I am talking about here.

I am promoting a form of organic mentoring, where the relationship comes together easily, through common interests and commitment and grows naturally. This mentor is someone invested in the mentee without any personal agenda or expectation for anything in return. The mentor is someone who has successfully walked his or her own professional path and shares the wisdom gained with the younger counterpart, maybe even preventing a repeat of errors and lessons learned the hard way. A mentor can clear the way of obstacles and guides rather than makes decisions. A good mentor is honest with you, even when it hurts.

If you are serious about having a maximally successful career, you owe it to yourself to find a good mentor. It can cut years off your learning process, possibly open doors, help you through the rough spots, and create greater success than you may have ever anticipated. It isn't necessary or maybe even possible to find someone who has the exact career you want to have, just find someone with a proven track record for success. Find the person who has achieved what you hope to achieve, someone you like and likes you, and someone who is willing to take the time to help. Once you have your mentor, you are already ahead of your competition. If you are really extra lucky, as I was, you too may end up with a lifelong dear friend.

What is an Expert?

I attend many continuing education conferences that all tend to be relatively similar, except for one recently where I heard something I've never heard before. The first speaker in one workshop gave a good presentation with valuable and thought-provoking information. The next workshop was with another speaker who proceeded to contradict, apparently unknowingly, much of what the last speaker had just presented. Both speakers were considered experts in the same field, both spoke with authority and confidence, and both were passionate on the topic. Which one was right?

It seems there is a hoard of "experts" on just about every subject you can imagine these days. The internet has given a voice to anyone interested in going public with an opinion. Some cable news programs now report viewers "Tweets" as newsworthy information. So many people with so many opinions, opinions they think need to be shared, are worthy of being shared, and maybe even that they have the right to share. Who do you believe? Who are the real experts, and how do you know if you've found one?

Real experts are not people who have all the answers. Experts are people who are well educated and make the effort to stay continuously informed in their area of specialty, and then give expert OPINIONS based on that foundation of knowledge. They are also the first to admit when they do not know some particular piece of information but likely offer to find out. Even lawyers and accountants who have endless laws and regulations to guide them are dealing with ever-changing rules and can disagree from one to the next and from one situation to another.

When I heard the two different speakers present conflicting information on a subject of importance to me in my work, I dug in and did my own homework. I looked closely at the credentials of the speakers, I read through all their literature and more, I spoke with multiple other sources on the same subject, and I looked at relevant cases of my own. Yes, it was a lot of extra work, but that's what experts do.

Silence Empowers Sexual Perpetrators

Whether it's the world of sports or the world of politics, sex-related scandals have become frequent and recurring headline news. I have worked with an endless number of cases involving every type of sexual assault and abuse imaginable, and some beyond imagination.

In my previous career as a Human Resources professional, it was my job to investigate claims of sexual harassment from the time the complaint first surfaced through to determining and implementing consequences. And, as a young corporate professional woman myself, I was the victim of sexual harassment. Today as a therapist, I bear witness to the stories of too many. I know this subject and I know it well.

My own experience involved both blatant verbal and physical assault, but it was the 80's and I did not see that I had any recourse if I wanted to keep my job. There were many days I got home from work and sat in my car and cried. When the same man blocked me from a promotion for a job I had actively been performing for many months, I'd had enough and sought legal counsel. The attorney told me he could see I had a promising future ahead of me and advised me to say nothing to protect that potential. That was the legal advice I got for my money. I ended up choosing the only acceptable option, and I left the organization and accepted a promotion somewhere else.

I could get on a soapbox here. I could get on a soapbox for people both unjustly accused and for people victimized. I could get on a soapbox about family members as well as schools and corporations and churches that protect known perpetrators. I could get on a soapbox for so many injured children who carry their wounds into adulthood, about women whose voices were stilled as their choices were smashed, and about men who were crippled by the shame of their assaults that too many say they should have been able to stop or worse yet enjoyed. I could get on a soapbox about how so many victims are the ones who get attacked, even in cases when there were witnesses to their assaults. I could get on a huge soap box about the arrogant and entitled bully perpetrators who get to go on with life unscathed as if they have done nothing wrong, and in fact may even believe they did nothing wrong. But, getting on my soapbox suggests that I have answers when in fact what I really have is questions, one in particular. What is it going to take for it to stop?

Fear of Failure

Who hasn't heard or participated in a discussion at some point or another about the fear of failure? It seems like a very straightforward term with clear definition, but I believe it is more often than not an entirely different issue simply camouflaged as something it is not. I believe fear of failure is far more often fear of success.

Decline promotions you earned at work because the timing is never quite right? Repeating pattern of relationships going incredibly well until there's a huge fight following a particularly intimate and happy time? One semester away from getting a degree and quit? Start up a successful business only to see it implode because of foolish or high risk choices?

The core issue behind fear of success is typically an underlying message of not being good enough—not good enough to get promoted, not good enough to be loved and have a lasting relationship, not good enough to graduate with a degree, not good enough to be a successful entrepreneur--not good enough to deserve good things and to be happy. The source of this negative programming originates in childhood and comes from an authority figure who delivers damaging messages repeatedly and over an extended period of time. Children don't have the ability to logically reason what might be behind the adult's behaviors and words. A child simply trusts that what they are being told is true and is left wondering, "What is wrong with me?"

I often talk with people who can explain to me in great detail all the reasons they fear failure, all the reasons they have failed, and all the bad things that will happen if they fail or fail again. On the other hand, when I ask what will happen if the outcome is success, I am often met with confused silence. Preparing for worst case scenarios is a prudent part of planning, but focusing on the big picture to create success can turn dreams into reality.

The Romance of a Business

As a professional with one foot in the world of mental health and the other in the world of business, I am a bit of an odd duck. In my work with people, relationships, businesses and careers, I have been fascinated by how similar the patterns and challenges are between these fields. Be it partnership challenges, communication difficulties, conflict resolutions, getting together or moving apart, the work has many parallels.

Just as a new love interest can tickle your fancy, so can the idea of a owning your own business. While infatuation is intoxicating stuff, it is not a good foundation for making solid long-term decisions. Our perspectives can be biased as things look better than they probably should and red flags get pushed aside. There is no challenge that cannot be overcome! We could talk for days and never need sleep or run out of more to say. Surely this was meant to be!

By all means, fall in love. Fall in love with the idea of owning and planning your own business. When else will you have so much energy, so much motivation and excitement? We love to fall in love, but even more, we need to fall in love. It is these intense emotions and good feelings, personally and professionally, that we need to get through some of the inevitably tough times ahead. This is just the beginning.

Now it's time to play devil's advocate, re-examining and challenging ideas until balanced thinking returns. Talk to every relevant business expert you can find to get professional opinions and advice. Avoid friends and relatives who are emotionally but not financially invested in your ideas. It's easy to get excited about someone else's new business when you have nothing at risk. Being nervous at this stage is part of the process, but being scared demands further examination.

Just like getting married requires a license and a legally binding contract, so does starting up a company. Often people feel that any question or anticipatory legal arrangement means they doubt the viability of the new venture or may imply they are not fully committed. Also, new starts ups, personal or business, may avoid involving any lawyers to reserve available funds as they see more money going out the door than is initially coming in.

It just makes good sense to get competent legal advice before signing anything in ink. Manage the attorney up front. Say how much you can afford to spend and specifically what advice you are looking to receive. Be clear about your current level of knowledge so you don't start out too simple and waste valuable time or too complicated and get overwhelmed with details. If the attorney is talking over your head or going too fast, stop and start over. You are the client and the one paying the bill. Ask for what you need and at the pace you need it. Any good attorney will be happy to comply.

Just as relationships grow and change over time, so do businesses. How the people involved commit, communicate, and handle conflict and uncertainty will play a major role in long-term success. Similar to marriage counseling, battles for power and control present the greatest challenges with the least satisfying outcomes. Agreeing to leave egos at the door and to work together as a team is a good plan, no matter what the relationship.

Even happy endings are endings, and of course, so are unhappy endings. Planning in advance, as early as the beginning, for how the desired ending will happen is smart. Whether you are a fan of prenuptial agreements or not, the fact is that a divorce with one is a whole lot faster, easier and cheaper than a nasty divorce without one.

A happy, loving, healthy marriage is a wonderful thing. A strong and successful business is pretty good, too. Both go through many stages from beginning to end, and demand nurturing and commitment to thrive. Neither succeeds by accident or chance or luck. Falling in love, with a person or an idea, is the magic that makes it all possible.

Burn Out on Steroids

Burn out tends to go with high level, high stress jobs and careers. There is an unspoken but widely accepted rule that lays the groundwork--show no weakness. Revealing vulnerabilities to employees, clients, customers, vendors, lenders or even family who all count on you is a luxury many feel they just can't afford. You may remember the old movie "All That Jazz." The lead character played by Roy Schneider, looking beaten and battered as he faces yet another day, gazes into his bathroom mirror and announces, "Show time!" It's kind of like that; some days it's a lot like that.

Burn out typically comes and goes but it seems burn out today has come and isn't leaving anytime soon. The determination it has taken to survive devastating economic trends while keeping pace with constantly changing technologies has left many business owners and professionals battling chronic bad moods, fatigue, tenuous relationships, health problems triggered or at least exacerbated by relentless stress, and not nearly enough time for fun. The professionals who have survived to do business another day are depleted, just when they need more energy and not less.

This group of people usually does a pretty good job of taking care of themselves. They tend to eat well, go to the gym, and have strong social outlets. What they tend not to be good at doing is taking breaks from their super human personae to just be vulnerable.

Some even chastise themselves for "doing nothing," an activity most refer to as "resting."

The Best Business Plan designed to continue success into the foreseeable future is to include finding someone you can trust, that you can tell "I'm tired" or "I'm scared" or "I'm angry" without risk of repercussion or breach of confidentiality. The relentless changes happening at near warp speed in the world are creating both opportunities and obstacles. The effects on careers and businesses are unprecedented and in many ways unpredictable, and not slowing down anytime soon. Those who embrace the changes and pace themselves carefully will be the ones who go the distance.

Sex Addiction or Just Busted?

Is there a growing epidemic of sex addiction? Or, are there just a growing number of people who are getting caught being unfaithful who claim to be sex addicts as a defense for their behavior choices?

It is a good policy not to comment or diagnose or label anyone or any situation without having all the facts, not to mention the professional competence. Answering vague or broad questions with specific answers tends to yield poor results. That being said, there are some facts that may offer some clarity on this complicated and controversial topic.

There is no doubt the internet has irreversibly changed and continues to change the world as we knew it. Even our language changes at lightning speed instead of over a generation. Hearing terms like "cybersex" and "sexting" only confuses this subject even more. So, what if we simply use real definitions? We know what they are. Like, sneaking around behind your partner's back to communicate with a third party is a BETRAYAL. Like, engaging in any sexual interaction without your partner's knowledge isn't "dating," it's CHEATING. Like, carelessly sending out X-rated photos of your private parts isn't Tweeting, it is CAREER SUICIDE.

There really are people who suffer and work hard to recover from true sex addiction, sometimes including in-patient treatment or "re-hab." When caught up in their addiction, these individuals engage in increasingly more dangerous activities compulsively, typically living at least a double life, headed down the road of self destruction. Their issue isn't an overactive libido, it is an underactive level of self esteem. It seems like people claiming addiction as a self-defense tactic may owe those working hard in their commitment to recovery a serious apology.

If you are using electronic devices of any kind in your underground activities, you can pretty much bet you are going to get caught. Maybe you even want to get caught. You might be too smart to say anything, but what about the social media posting from the cutie you met last night who turns out to be "Friends" with your next door neighbor? How do you explain that flurry of incriminating text messages when you were taking the dog out for a long midnight walk?

In an attempt to mitigate damages, it is a common to hear the offender attempt to minimize the harm caused by saying there was no actual physical contact or sexual consummation since interaction was only online. If a person is keeping his or her behavior secret from a committed partner, and it isn't to plan a surprise birthday party, the act is one of infidelity. The secrecy puts the partner unknowingly in a relationship where only half of the couple is fully present, engaged and acting in good faith.

As difficult as it is may be to believe, there can be healthy recovery in these types of situations, for individuals and for relationships, but it doesn't come easily and it doesn't come fast. A skilled therapist can be a powerful ally bringing in some objectivity, introducing new ideas, and facilitating interactions with a fresh perspective. Changing behaviors is hard, but continuing destructive behaviors come with a consequence that can be even harder.

The Tao of Sportsmanship

Whether you are dealing with little league baseball, college football, competing in the Olympics, or running around the ring in a dog show, the way we win and the way we lose says more about the character of the participant than it does about the sport.

It is no great revelation that winning is more fun than losing. Who would participate in any sport if they didn't want and believe they could win? Winning comes with the adrenaline rush, the spotlight, the moment of fame, and most of all the coveted affirmation that you and/or yours are the best of the best.

Winning with grace is a subject that seems to get lost in all the chaos and excitement, but maybe it should get its own share of the spotlight. In competitive sports, every single person, every single team that wins does so because others did not. Whether it happens a little or it happens a lot, if you are the winner you are in a position to demonstrate grace and gratitude by acknowledging that without competition there would be no winners.

Of course for every winner there has to be, to be blunt, at least one loser. Losing with dignity, congratulating your competition with sincerity despite disappointment requires strength, courage, and a whole lot of class. Committing to learn from the loss in order to increase the odds of a different outcome next time demands determination, devotion and tenacity, perhaps the real description of a "winner."

Maybe you are somewhere in the middle, no longer a rookie but not yet in the winner's circle. If you are working hard but not where you want to be, focus on what you've done well so you can do it more, and learn from your mistakes so you can do better. Too often people get so hung up on what isn't going well that they forget to pay attention to what is. Knowing the difference is a smart advantage.

If you are new to your sport, full of enthusiasm and ambition, work diligently to educate yourself. Watch everyone around you knowing that teachers come in many forms, and we can learn from them all. Jump in sooner than later. You will make mistakes and you will feel foolish, just like everyone else when they started—and maybe well after they started.

Regardless of what sport you are in or where you are in it, enjoy meeting people who share your interests and your passions. What a perfect way to make new friends, learn from each other, celebrate your successes and lament your losses. Winning may be more fun than losing, but winning with friends cheering you on is the best fun of all.

Afterword

Don't Give up on Your Dreams

If you asked me what the best moment of my childhood was, I could tell you without hesitation. As a young girl caught in the war zone of my parents' acrimonious divorce, the moment I found magic will always stand out in my mind. It was the day I went to my first dog show.

It was a beautiful summer day when I walked onto the show grounds. To my immediate left, I saw Afghan Hounds gliding effortlessly around the ring, hair flowing back elegantly and their feet never appearing to touch the ground. I was instantly in love. As I walked further, I saw amazing dogs everywhere I looked, and I wanted at least one of each. The feeling was intoxicating, overwhelming. I was happy and nothing else mattered.

I never stopped going to dog shows from that day on. I never stopped wanting to be the one in the ring with my own gorgeous dog, but John Lennon was right when he said, "Life is what happens while you're making other plans." College, raising a family, creating careers and businesses didn't leave much time for my dream that refused to die.

When the day finally arrived that I had the freedom and the luxury to start my dog show career, I was coming into the sport late and behind all those who had many years of experience. I needed a mentor but had no clue where to find one, or what to even ask if I did find one. Learning things the hard way takes a lot more time than the opposite and tends to include much more disappointment, at least that's how it worked for me. Finding a show-worthy dog proved to be much more difficult than I ever imagined. I ended up with some wonderful family pets, one great therapy dog, but no champions in the house.

Most people would probably have given up, but giving up is never something I have been good at doing. I just needed a better strategy, and there was no more time to lose. I went to work. I gave myself credit for what I did know and got busy figuring out what I didn't. I read and I read some more. I talked to everyone who would talk to me. I went to many shows dog-less and continued to watch and learn. I risked trusting people I didn't really know, exposing my own lack of knowledge in order to grow and succeed, and the risks ultimately paid off. I promised myself I would in turn offer help in the future to others getting started in a pay-it-forward kind of way.

I do not believe dreams come true by accident or luck. I believe dreams come true through perseverance, determination and hard work. A touch of that magic I mentioned doesn't hurt and I found it for the second time on a cold clear day in Chicago late in 2011. Surrounded by new friends, many adorable puppies, and a yummy feast of great food, I looked at one little 10-week-old puppy and thought to myself, "This is the one I've been looking for all my life." Hours later, our plane landed and the new addition met her new family as our adventure together began.

Somehow, some way, deep down inside I knew as that little girl that the day would come when it would be me in the ring with my own beautiful dog. Call it intuition, call it tenacity, call it whatever, I just knew. What I didn't know and never could have imagined then was that when the day finally arrived, my girl gliding along at one end of the leash and me at the other, that my children and their children would be cheering us on from ring side as we crossed the line to Champion and my dream of a lifetime came true. I never gave up on my dream. Don't give up on yours.

The future belongs to those who believe in the beauty of their dreams – Eleanor Roosevelt